Close up on Psychology

Supplemental Readings
From the *APA Monitor*

Edited by

Jill N. Reich,

Elizabeth Q. Bulatao,

Gary R. VandenBos, and

Rhea K. Farberman

AMERICAN PSYCHOLOGICAL ASSOCIATION
WASHINGTON, DC

Published by
American Psychological Association
750 First Street, NE
Washington, DC 20002

Copies may be ordered from
APA Order Department
P.O. Box 92984
Washington, DC 20090-2984

In the UK and Europe, copies may be ordered from
American Psychological Association
3 Henrietta Street
Covent Garden, London
WC2E 8LU England

Typeset in Futura and New Baskerville by EPS Group Inc., Easton, MD

Cover designer: Minker Design, Bethesda, MD
Printer: Edwards Brothers, Inc., Ann Arbor, MI
Technical/production editor: Susan Bedford

Library of Congress Cataloging-in-Publication Data

Close up on psychology : supplemental readings from the APA monitor / edited by
  Jill N. Reich ... [et al.].
    p.   cm.
  ISBN 1-55798-427-1 (alk. paper)
  1. Psychology.   I. Reich, Jill Nagy.   II. APA monitor.
BF121.C525   1997
150—dc21   97-10904
                                                                           CIP

British Library Cataloguing-in-Publication Data
A CIP record is available from the British Library

Printed in the United States of America
First edition

Contents

Preface

Psychology is typically defined as the scientific study of behavior and mental processes. Let us consider this definition carefully, as there are some important elements in it.

First, psychology is a *science*. This initially may seem to be an odd notion to you, because psychology in your school may be in the social studies department, or the word *science* may conjure up images of test tubes and dissections. Actually, both of these images are partially correct and partially incorrect in reference to psychology. Psychology is a behavioral science. This means that it deals with social behavior such as prejudice, personal behavior such as personality development, and biological behavior such as how the nervous system affects our functioning and how what we do affects our nervous system. But, subject matter aside, psychology is a science because it uses the scientific method in its efforts to understand, explain, and predict how organisms behave and think. Some might say that the answers to questions about how people behave and think are just common sense, but, as you learn more about psychology, you will begin to realize that many things that we assume to be true, because they are common sense, are neither common nor sensical. These "truths" simply do not hold up in the face of scientific investigation. This is one of the most exciting things about psychology. It grabs our attention with its questions, and leads us to answers and conclusions we may not have anticipated.

A second important element in the definition of psychology is *behavior*. Behavior can be either overt (easily and openly observable) or covert (internal and less readily apparent). Modern technology allows researchers to observe and measure a much wider range of behaviors than was previously possible. These behaviors include brain activity, reaction time measured in milliseconds, and even communication between cells in the nervous system. This increased ability to observe and measure a wide range of behaviors has made it possible to scientifically study such topics as memory, emotions, problem solving, language development, and the biological components of mental disorders.

Another important element in the definition of psychology is *mental processes*, or *cognitions*. These include how organisms think, perceive, feel, anticipate, solve problems, and mentally structure their worlds. Cognitions play an important role in understanding social interactions, learning and memory, decision making, coping behaviors, attitudes, and so forth.

Many people, when psychology is mentioned, think of clinical psychologists, primarily as psychotherapists. This is, in fact, a major area of activity in psychology. Over 60,000 doctoral level professional psychologists conduct various forms of psychotherapy with individuals, couples, families, and groups addressing mental or emotional disorders and behavioral problems. However, this is only one aspect of psychology.

The American Psychological Association (APA) is made up of 51 divisions, each one devoted to a more in depth understanding of a specific aspect of behavior. These include such diverse interests as industrial and organizational psychology, educational psychology, infant and child development, adult development and aging, learning and memory, psychopharmacology, neuropsychology, health psychology, and many more areas. Within each of these specific areas, researchers and educators are actively involved in learning new things and applying that new information. This is the other side of psychology, the psychological scientist who is somewhat less familiar to the average person.

Psychologists share their research findings by publishing reports in professional journals. Fortunately for those of us who do not have the time or expertise to read many of these reports, the APA publishes a newspaper, the *APA Monitor*, which presents information about current topics in psychology in clear, straightforward language. These articles tend to be highly readable, informative, and most of all interesting. They help the reader to see the "real world" of psychology. This book is a collection of some of the best articles that have appeared in the *Monitor*. There is a wide range of topics covered, and they are organized in a fashion similar to that found in most introductory psychology textbooks.

As you read through the table of contents, you will see over and over how the scientific work of psychology is far from dry; you'll see how it touches every aspect of life experience. We hope that the readings in this book give you a better understanding of the discipline of psychology; a deeper insight into your own behavior, thoughts, and emotions; and an appreciation of the complex interplay of variables that shape the world in which we live.

Our thanks to the high school teachers whose ideas sparked this reader and whose enthusiasm ensured its production. Two individuals were central to, first the idea, and, later, the implementation of this book—namely, Ludy T. Benjamin, Jr., and Carol Dean, respectively. Organizationally, the development of this volume was supported and nurtured by the Executive Board of TOPSS (Teachers of Psychology in Secondary Schools) and the individuals who served on that Board over the last several years.

1

Sensation, Perception, and Neuroscience

Research Explores Complexity of Taste

Beth Azar

Without the ability to taste, eating would certainly be less of a pleasure and more a mere necessity. But taste provides humans more than just the capacity to enjoy their food. Flavors cause chemical reactions in the mouth that extend into the brain and that can affect behavior and bodily function.

Although the four basic tastes—salt, bitter, sweet, and sour—were identified hundreds of years ago, researchers are only now discovering some subtle mysteries about how people taste and what makes tasting such a complex phenomenon with many implications.

An Inherited Trait?

All tasters are not created equal. Researchers have known for years that some people can taste certain substances that others either can't taste at all or taste less strongly. Two main indicators of taste proclivity are the bitter compounds phenylthiocarbamide, or PTC, and 6-n-propyl-thiouracil, or PROP. To "super-tasters," these compounds taste incredibly bitter, to "non-tasters" they have no taste, and to "middle-tasters" they are moderately bitter.

Psychologist Linda Bartoshuk, PhD, of Yale University School of Medicine, and her colleagues have recently correlated taste proclivity to number of taste buds. Super-tasters not only have taste buds that taste PTC and PROP, they have more taste buds, which causes them to taste many flavors, including bitter and sweet, more intensely than other people.

Bartoshuk suspects, and she said preliminary evidence supports, that taste proclivity is an inherited trait: Super-tasters inherit two dom-

From the *APA Monitor*, November 1994, p. 21.

inant genes, moderate tasters inherit one dominant and one recessive gene, and non-tasters inherit two recessive genes. Such differences give a new perspective to taste preferences. A moderate-tasting or non-tasting parent may need to develop more tolerance for the dislikes of a super-tasting child. Bartoshuk hopes to do more work with food preferences and perhaps look at correlations between taste proclivity and weight.

Pain Sensitivity

The number of taste buds also correlates to the number of pain receptors on the tongue, said Bartoshuk. When people eat spicy food, the spicy taste results from the activation of pain fibers that are wrapped around taste fibers in the taste buds. Capsaicin, a chemical found in most types of hot pepper, triggers more pain for super-tasters than for non-tasters because of the extra fibers.

Barry Green, PhD, of the Monell Chemical Senses Center in Philadelphia, has been trying to find links between the pain system and other senses. His work with capsaicin has shown that people can become desensitized to the pain caused by the chemical. If capsaicin is applied to the tongue and the pain is allowed to dissipate naturally, when the chemical is applied again, the person will feel no pain.

Bartoshuk has used this idea to help chemotherapy patients deal with painful mouth sores. She gave the patients hard candies containing capsaicin, triggering the burn in the mouth from a spicy meal. When the burning died down after about 20 minutes, not only had the burn of the candy disappeared but so had the pain from the sores.

"The desensitization works on the pain itself, not on the lesions," Bartoshuk explained.

The Neurochemical Angle

An intriguing new finding from the neurochemical angle comes from the work of psychologist Bartley Hoebel, PhD, on the biochemical mechanisms of eating. Hoebel and his colleagues at Princeton University have produced the first evidence of conditioned neurotransmitter release, he said.

Just as Pavlov's dogs salivated at the ringing of a bell, the rats' brains in Hoebel's study released dopamine in response to a flavor.

Eating normally causes the brain to release dopamine, a process that is known to reinforce behavior.

Hoebel and his colleagues gave rats a flavor paired with food and got the standard dopamine release. They then took away the food and administered only the flavor—and dopamine release continued.

If the rats "taste a flavor that reminds them of nutrition in the stomach, that flavor will release dopamine," said Hoebel.

Conversely, "a flavor paired with nausea decreases dopamine release" and also increases levels of the neurotransmitter acetylcholine— a chemical that has been found to inhibit eating. Such a response provides a conditioned taste aversion, Hoebel said.

Such conditioning implies that the chemical reward and warning system that is triggered during eating can be triggered by taste alone. Such a system could be part of an eating learning system that regulates what people eat and when they eat it, said Hoebel.

Why Is It That Practice Makes Perfect?

Beth Azar

Practice may not always make you perfect, but it is likely to make a lasting impression on your brain.

Two new brain studies have found that repetitive motor sequences can trigger changes in the parts of the brain that accept sensory information and control motor function. These changes may explain why coordination and ability improve with practice on tasks such as typing and playing an instrument.

This research adds another dimension to a growing body of work on brain plasticity—the brain's ability to alter its circuitry—by finding unexpected reorganization associated with developing advanced motor skills.

Extra Brain Resources

Psychologists have long noted that, with practice, people can learn a complex motor task—such as rapid sequences of finger movements—and improve their speed and accuracy until they plateau at a certain performance level. But the performance doesn't transfer to learning other, similar sequences—such as another piano tune—only to the one that's been practiced.

That's because the brain uses more space, which presumably provides more "power," to perform the practiced sequence, according a new study by psychologists Avi Karni, MD, PhD, and Leslie Ungerleider, PhD, of the Laboratory of Neuropsychology at the National Institute of Mental Health and their colleagues at the National Institutes of Health.

From the *APA Monitor*, January 1996, p. 18.

Karni and Ungerleider measured brain activity once a week for five weeks in the primary motor cortex of six men who performed two different but highly similar finger-tapping sequences at a set pace. Each subject practiced one sequence 10 to 20 minutes each day but performed the other sequence only during the testing sessions.

During these sessions, the researchers measured brain activity using functional magnetic resonance imaging—a scanning technique that measures the amount of blood oxygen in specific brain regions. After five weeks, the researchers found that tapping the practiced sequence activated a larger portion of the motor cortex than tapping the other sequence. The changes remained a year later as did superior performance on the practiced sequence, with no practice in the intervening time, said Ungerleider.

These results indicate that changes occur in the primary motor cortex as a result of learning, she said. But it is not a generalizable kind of learning: It's specific to one sequence of movements. That's why Ungerleider thinks the brain may set up larger-than-normal expert circuits to handle specific, practiced sequences of movements.

The kind of learning this study looked at is procedural learning, or learning that people don't have to consciously recollect, such as driving a car or riding a bike, Ungerleider explained. It is also the type of knowledge that is negatively affected in people with brain disorders, such as in late stages of Alzheimer's disease.

Although researchers are still trying to uncover the basics about how the brain learns and remembers, scientists hope that the basic knowledge will some day have clinical significance for treating such disorders, she said.

The Somatosensory Cortex

Other researchers have found similar changes in the somatosensory cortex—the part of the brain that receives sensory information from all parts of the body.

Michael Merzenich, PhD, of the University of California-San Diego, stimulated one or two fingers of monkeys repeatedly over a few weeks. He then measured activity in the somatosensory cortex of the monkeys as he lightly brushed the same fingers. He found that the amount of space activated in the part of the somatosensory cortex that represents the fingers was bigger than that for the other fingers.

To see if the same principle applies to humans, psychologists Thomas Elbert, PhD, of the University of Konstanz in Germany, Edward Taub, PhD, of the University of Alabama at Birmingham and colleagues recently examined the brains of stringed-instrument players. String players use their left-hand fingers considerably more than their right-hand fingers. They also use them considerably more than the average person. The researchers theorized that if repeated stimulation of a body part causes a change in the brain, the change would be evident in the area of the brain that receives information from the left-hand fingers of these musicians.

The researchers' subjects included six violinists, two cellists, and a guitarist as well as six nonmusician controls. Using a technique called magnetic source imaging, the researchers measured brain activity in the somatosensory cortex of the subjects while applying a light touch to their fingers. Touching the string players' left fingers activated a larger area of the cortex than it did for the nonmusicians.

The effect was greatest for subjects who started playing a stringed instrument before age 13, but it was also quite dramatic for those who started later. That makes sense, said Taub: The brain is certainly more capable of change early in development. But what's remarkable is that the brain is still quite plastic in adults, something not commonly believed 10 years ago, he said.

The study didn't address whether the extra brain space devoted to the fingers improves playing in general, but the researchers presume the amount of room the brain devotes to the motion is somehow beneficial. It may be that this expansion in the somatosensory cortex improves general dexterity, while the expansion Ungerleider saw in the motor cortex improves performance on a specific series of movements.

In practical terms, Ungerleider may have found the mechanism by which a string player learns a new piece of music and can, years after learning it, still play with the same proficiency. Taub and his colleagues may also have found the mechanism by which the string player's fingers develop the proficiency to move.

Both results are intriguing, said Tim Pons, PhD, of Bowman Gray School of Medicine, but he's not sure they mean the brain is reorganizing. Instead, Pons posits that it's probably a competition among different parts of the brain to capture more space for these functions. People who start playing violin later in life can capture some extra space for their fingers, but not the same amount available to young people, he explained.

That may be true, said Ungerleider. But the data do indicate plasticity; the brain is adapting and adjusting to experience, even in adults. And if the mechanism behind that plasticity can be tapped, researchers may begin to understand and combat all kinds of learning-related disorders, from learning disabilities to brain damage-related deficits.

Musical Studies Provide Clues to Brain Functions

Beth Azar

By the time Beethoven completed his final symphony he couldn't hear a note of it. The music he wrote was all in his head.

Remarkable? Yes. But not only because he was a genius. Also extraordinary was Beethoven's ability to hear melodies without really hearing them—to imagine songs, made up or recalled. This skill is one of many that fascinates psychologists and neuroscientists interested in how people make and process music. The human brain, they believe, seems designed to create, perceive, process, and recall songs as easily as language. Indeed, virtually every culture makes music using a well-structured system of tones and rhythms.

By looking at the brain, these researchers hope to tease apart how people perceive music, understand it, and play it in their heads and with their hands. Researchers are developing neural net models, studying people with brain damage who have lost some musical abilities, and using advanced brain imaging technologies to piece together what parts of the brain carry out which music-related functions.

A Musical Template

Music is built from simple parts. Natural sounds contain air molecules vibrating at different frequencies. Certain frequency combinations are associated with pitches—how high or low a note sounds. A sequence of pitches constitutes a melody and a simultaneous combination of tone

From the *APA Monitor*, April 1996, pp. 1, 24.

pitches makes up a chord, the basic element of harmony. The timing of sound events constitutes rhythm.

So it's not surprising that the inner ear—the first stop for sound—breaks down natural sounds into their component frequencies. What is striking is that the neurons lined up along the snail-like cochlea of the inner ear are organized like piano keys going from low to high frequencies: Different neurons encode different frequencies depending on their location in the cochlea. The 30,000 or so auditory nerve fibers of each human ear pass this frequency information to neurons in the brain stem, and from there the information gets passed to higher centers and, ultimately, the auditory cortex, where the conscious experience of sound takes shape.

As in the ear, neurons in the auditory cortex are arranged in order by frequency. Although it's not proven, one model of music perception posits that another set of neurons should recognize certain groups of frequencies as individual tones. A third set should then encode groups of tones as chords, says psychologist Jamshed Bharucha, PhD, who has been working on a neural network of music perception. He believes the neurons learn to recognize tones and chords from the musical structure in their environment.

"We live in a musical culture," said Bharucha, professor of psychology at Dartmouth College. "Music is around us from early on and neurons organize themselves in response to that musical structure."

Some of that structure is universal, such as the frequencies and tones people recognize. And some is specific to the culture someone lives in, said Bharucha. For example, the chords in Western music differ from those in Indian music. Bharucha believes people's brains develop special connections that help them recognize the chords of their culture.

Such a musical template in the brain might explain how people can imagine music in their heads as Beethoven did. A recent study by McGill University psychologist Robert Zatorre, PhD, and colleagues found that when people "hear" a song in their mind, the brain uses the same circuitry it uses to hear a song with their ears. This indicates that the brain doesn't need the sound waves to reproduce the sound.

"The same portion of the brain is being used when people imagine as when they hear, but [the sound is] being driven from the inside," said Zatorre. The brain must reconstruct the song using memory and neurons in the auditory cortex.

Mapping the Brain

Some people can't recognize a song enough to reproduce it out loud or in their heads: They have amusia, a rare disorder caused by damage in similar spots on both sides of the auditory cortex. The damage sometimes prevents patients from recognizing familiar songs but spares their ability to discern voices, traffic noise, and animal sounds, according to University of Montreal psychologist Isabelle Peretz, PhD.

She's studied three people with amusia. Although they say they enjoy music, they can't say if a tune is Beethoven's "Fifth Symphony" or "Jingle Bells." Furthermore, the damage appears to affect just melody recognition; the three patients can easily recall a rhythm and can dance and tap out a beat. This implies that people process melody and rhythm separately, Peretz said.

These studies tell us a lot about how people process music, said Peretz. It's obvious that there are specific areas of the brain that control our understanding and ability to recognize and process music. But the science of mapping musical functions of the brain is largely incomplete. Researchers estimate there may be up to 12 distinct regions in the auditory cortex that control music perception on each side of the brain, says neurobiologist Mark Tramo, PhD, of Harvard Medical School. It remains unknown what musical roles these anatomical regions play.

Because many aspects of language are housed on the left side of the brain, researchers seek to determine if one side of the brain has more control over musical understanding than another. Several studies suggest that the right hemisphere controls perception of pitch. But other research indicates that both sides of the brain have a role in perceiving music.

Zatorre has found that people with damaged right auditory cortices have trouble judging if one pitch is higher than another. People with similar damage to their left auditory cortex don't have this problem. He confirmed these results using the brain scanning technique positron emission tomography (PET), which measures brain activity: When subjects without brain damage judge pitch changes, a region on the brain's right side is active.

Tramo and Bharucha have evidence from studies of split-brain patients that people perceive tonal harmony principally with the right side of their brains. Surgery for some neurological disorders severs the connection between the right and left brain hemispheres of people with "split brains." Because the two sides can no longer communicate, researchers can study them separately.

Tramo and Bharucha found that the left hemisphere of split-brain patients had trouble judging if notes played together were harmonious or not, while their right hemispheres performed normally. But the same patients could use either their right or left hemispheres to recognize different musical instruments by their timbre.

"The jury is still out," said Tramo. "But it looks like lateralization isn't as strong for music as for language. Still, it is fascinating that the so-called 'minor' hemisphere might play a leading role in certain aspects of music perception and cognition."

This is only one of the many mysteries facing researchers interested in music and the brain. Just as the scientists in Beethoven's time mapped the mathematical relationships between an instrument's string length and how the string sounded when it was plucked, psychologists and neuroscientists are teasing apart the relationships among the auditory neurons in their effort to encode music.

Damaged Area of Brain Can Reorganize Itself

Beth Azar

Most of us grew up with an image of the brain as a hard-wired, unchangeable mass of cells. The basic circuitry was laid down before we were born, and if you lost a cell or two, it wouldn't grow back.

But over the past 10 to 15 years, neuroscientists and psychologists have debunked that theory, finding the adult brain much more "plastic"—able to rewire its circuitry in order to perform tasks that the brain was incapable of previously doing due to a severe injury or the amputation of a limb.

Over the next 10 to 20 years, the clinical implications of this research will be dramatic for people with brain damage that affects specific bodily functions, according to Tim Pons, PhD, in the department of neurosurgery at the Bowman Gray School of Medicine. Once researchers understand the mechanism of brain reorganization, they may be able to stimulate or manipulate the process and force brain areas to take over the lost functions.

Losing the Senses

Sensory information from all over the body is sent to the brain's somatosensory cortex. When we touch an object, the sensory nerves in our fingers trigger a response in a corresponding section of the somatosensory cortex. Researchers have mapped each body part to a specific section of the somatosensory cortex.

If damage severs the sensory connection between a body part and its sensory nerves, we can no longer feel the body part. Researchers

From the *APA Monitor*, January 1996, pp. 18, 19.

historically believed the damaged part of the brain would lie dormant. Now, research has begun to paint an image of a more plastic brain.

Among the first to challenge the idea of a hard-wired adult brain were Michael Merzenich, PhD, and his colleagues at the University of California-San Diego. In a 1983 experiment, they amputated a single finger of a monkey, severing its sensory connection with the brain. A small portion—one to two millimeters—of the disconnected cortex started receiving information from the adjacent fingers. Merzenich concluded that the adult brain could reorganize, but only on a small, incomplete scale.

In two follow-up studies on monkeys in the early 1990s, Pons, then at the National Institutes of Health, and his colleagues disconnected the sensory link between the brain and a hand and then an entire arm by cutting the sensory nerves at the spinal cord. In both studies, they found massive reorganization within the cortex when they looked at images of brain activity in the animals, he said.

In the second study, the researchers examined monkeys that had their sensory nerves on one arm severed from the cortex 12 years earlier. This ensured that any and all reorganization had already occurred, said Pons.

In the cortex of monkeys and humans, sensory input from the arm goes to an area of the somatosensory cortex sandwiched between the areas that receive sensory information from the torso and the face. So the researchers measured activity in the monkeys' somatosensory cortex while they lightly brushed the monkeys' faces and abdomens. They were astounded to find that the entire region representing the upper limb responded to stimulation to the face, said Pons. It was 10 to 14 millimeters of reorganization, a level up to 10 times larger than what Merzenich saw.

Studies on Humans

To follow up on these results, one of Pons's co-authors, psychologist Edward Taub, PhD, of the University of Alabama at Birmingham, joined colleagues Thomas Elbert, PhD, Herta Flor, PhD, and others in Germany to look at humans who had had an arm amputated for medical reasons.

They again found massive cortical reorganization—the area once representing the lower arm accepted stimulation from the face as well as the amputation stump. This cortical invasion of the face into a brain area that had once been stimulated by the arm correlates with a phenomenon heard in 100-year-old anecdotes: People with an amputated arm often feel a sensation in a "phantom limb"—the amputated limb—when they touch their faces. Indeed, when researcher V. Ramachandran, PhD, lightly touched the faces of people who had had an arm amputated, they felt the sensation on their face and on a phantom limb. The amputees felt the same sensation when Ramachandran dribbled water on their faces.

Although it would be easy to assume that these sensations result from the "invasion" by the face of the brain area once stimulated by the amputated arm, Taub and colleagues have not found that there is such a connection. Even so, Pons believes Ramachandran's findings provide an interesting look at how the brain receives and processes information.

Even though the face is sending sensory information to the brain, the mind believes the arm—one that doesn't exist—is sending the information. Therefore, an intermediate part of the central-nervous system (CNS) must change the signal coming from the face to make it appear to be coming from the arm.

Pons is trying to locate the intermediary spot in the CNS where the transformation occurs. He's particularly interested in a phenomenon seen in people who suffer from phantom pain or chronic pain from cancer. If surgeons cut off the sensory input in one spot, another part of the brain seems to take over and the pain returns. Eventually, researchers should find the part of the brain that controls the perception of pain, Pons believes.

Taub has scientifically linked cortical reorganization to phantom-limb pain. He and his colleagues recently found that the more cortical reorganization that occurs in a person with an amputated arm, the more phantom-limb pain a person feels. This finding is the first to demonstrate a specific central-nervous system contribution to the experience of phantom limb pain, said Taub.

More generally, the findings are the first to show that cortical reorganization in adults has measurable, meaningful effects on perception and behavior, said Taub. And although phantom-limb pain is a disadvantageous outcome, it opens the possibility of an advantageous outcome—perhaps the recovery of function after a stroke, he explained.

2 Learning and Memory

Solving a Classic Visual Search Problem

Beth Azar

When a professional quarterback bungles a pass, spectators often question his vision or his brains.

But human factors psychologists Arthur Fisk, PhD, and Neff Walker, PhD, view the quarterback's plight as "a classic visual search problem" and blame a lack of training, not a lack of smarts. Capitalizing on skills-training research, the two Georgia Institute of Technology researchers have designed a computer-based training system to help quarterbacks choose the right receiver.

A Lack of Practice

Like many armchair spectators, Walker once wondered how quarterbacks could make so many poor and inaccurate throws. Then he learned how seldom they practice each play and it began to make sense. For any specific offensive play against a certain defense, a quarterback may only have a few hours of actual practice. Each season they get at most a few hundred hours of practice with only a small percentage spent practicing with full offensive and defensive teams. Often, a quarterback will face a particular play for the first time during an actual game.

From previous research on skill acquisition, Fisk and Walker knew that to improve at a visual search task, people require thousands of practice trials. In support of this, the average age of the National Football League's (NFL) best quarterbacks is 34, making it the only position where age—and presumably amount of practice—makes a difference.

From the *APA Monitor*, July 1996, p. 20.

Picking Apart a Pass

To design any type of training system, researchers must identify the elements of each task that are consistent from trial to trial, said Fisk. With help from a college football coach, he and Walker defined four primary cognitive and perceptual components of a quarterback's decision to throw the ball:

1. Once the coach specifies the offensive play, the quarterback must remember the pattern each of several receivers is expected to run.
2. Before the quarterback receives the ball, he must scan the defense and determine what defensive set it's in.
3. Given the play and the defensive set, the quarterback must remember which receiver to look at first, second, third, and so on (the order is determined in advance based on who is most likely to be open).
4. After the snap, the quarterback must look at each receiver in turn and determine which one is "open," and then throw the ball to that receiver.

These four tasks fit into two categories: retrieval tasks, which include remembering the pass patterns and receiver-read sequences; and perceptual judgment tasks, which include recognizing the defensive set and judging which receiver is open. Earlier research showed that training can improve these two types of tasks and that they can become "automatic"—the goal of training.

Research on training in the 1970s and 1980s by Fisk, Walter Schneider, PhD, and Richard Schiffrin, PhD, found that visual search skills can become automated, or unconscious, after many repetitions.

"If you can automatize critical components of a critical skill, you can develop performance that is fast, error-resistant, and fluid," said Fisk.

He and Walker wanted to design a training system that would give quarterbacks enough practice choosing the correct receiver to make each aspect of the process automatic.

Video Learning

The computer-based training system Fisk and Walker developed displays film clips of actual game and scrimmage plays on a large-screen digitized video system. The video shows the playing field from a vantage point just behind the quarterback, providing a view of all the offensive and defensive players.

Giving a training quarterback a view similar to what he'd see on the field helps quarterbacks develop automatic responses to the visual stimuli they'll see during actual play—the look of the defense, the movement of players, explained Walker. Viewing plays from the sidelines—where most teams shoot their video—helps players understand a play, but doesn't cultivate automatic responses to the images, he said.

Each video clip lasts six to eight seconds, from the time the players break out of the huddle until the play ends. Using a control panel the size of a computer keyboard, a quarterback watches the play and, using buttons on the keyboard, selects the receiver he would throw the ball to. (The quarterback on screen might throw to the right or wrong receiver, so the trainee must make his own judgment.)

The system responds with a "beep" for a correct choice and a "buzz" for an incorrect choice. It then gives feedback on the speed and accuracy of the choice and provides additional information on the defensive set and the correct read sequence.

Quarterbacks can also practice individual components of the passing task, such as deciding which order to look at the receivers. The system again gives feedback on the speed and accuracy of his response.

Giving immediate feedback is crucial, said Walker: If feedback comes long after the play is over—which happens often during actual practices—the quarterback can't integrate it into his memory of that play.

Trainees can practice the same play over and over, or several different plays in succession. And coaches can create a program that allows a quarterback to practice plays that might come up later with a real opponent, explained Walker.

If a quarterback practices for 30 minutes a day, five days a week, he can get more than 30,000 repetitions in six months, said Walker. "It would take 10 to 15 years of regular practice and play to get this many repetitions."

It's hard to tell whether the system actually improves quarterbacks' performance, said Walker. The Georgia Tech football team used the system for two years and the NFL's Atlanta Falcons used it last year, to rave reviews by coaches and quarterbacks. However, there's no way to measure in-play performance in a controlled way.

"Too many other factors determine how well a quarterback does his job," Walker said. There's no controlling how well the defense is playing, how well the offense is playing, or how well the coach is calling the play.

However, he and Fisk are testing if the same kind of system leads to automatic response in the lab, using computerized "X"s and "O"s to represent football players on opposite teams. They also want to determine whether quarterbacks will learn better if the video-training system highlights the players they should watch more closely.

Meanwhile, they've given the system to TREK Sports, a company owned by ex-football coach Craig Cason. TREK Sports is working with the NFL to hone the device and hopes to eventually sell it to teams. Fisk and Walker don't expect it will create superstars from mediocre players. But they hope it can give extra practice to second- and third-string players, who get less time on the field than first stringers.

"If we can help a quarterback make two or three better decisions per game, it might make a big difference," said Walker. "If Pittsburgh's man [Neil O'Donnell] threw only one instead of two interceptions during the Superbowl, it might have saved the game for them."

Children Can Excel When They Learn From Mistakes

Bridget Murray

Children's performance in school may stem largely from their attitudes toward failure, and their reactions to their own failure, says a Columbia University psychologist.

Children who equate failing an exam with being innately incapable are more likely to give up on their academics. But those who see it as a signal to study harder usually do better next time, explained Carol Dweck, PhD.

A veteran researcher of motivation and personality, Dweck has spent the past 20 years exploring children's helpless versus mastery approaches to their school work. She's found that children's views on learning and intelligence influence the two different thinking patterns. Lately Dweck has studied how those patterns originate, a key area for teachers and parents trying to motivate children and break them of the cycle of helplessness.

In a recent study of 107 kindergarten students in New York City, Dweck confirmed the notion that negative reactions to failure and criticism start early. Dweck asked the children to role-play a scene in which they pretended to give their teacher a gift they had made. Almost all of them were happy with the gift they gave. But, after the teacher found something wrong with it, nearly half of them decided that the gift they had made was "bad," while the rest of them still considered the gift "good."

The bad-gift group considered themselves unable to make a good gift and more often saw their inadequacy as a fixed trait than the good-gift group. That pessimistic view hurts academic motivation later on, Dweck says. She believes kindergarten teachers can help stop this pat-

From the *APA Monitor*, November 1995, p. 42.

tern by encouraging students to view their actions differently instead of judging their work as good or bad.

Entity Versus Incremental Theory

As Dweck's past research suggests, children who internalize messages of failure develop a warped view of their capability, and of intelligence in general. They have what she calls an "entity theory"—they believe people are born smart.

Alternatively, children who follow the "incremental theory" believe people have to seek knowledge and challenges to become smart. Incremental theorists are mastery-oriented and focus on learning and effort.

Entity theorists are performance-oriented and focus on passing or failing, says Dweck. When they fail they often think they're incapable and give up. Meanwhile incremental theorists forge ahead, viewing their failures as a learning process that expands their intelligence.

"Kids who think intelligence is fixed become consumed with worry about whether they'll be judged smart or not," said Dweck. "Kids who think it's fluid don't worry so much and appreciate the long-term benefits of what they're actually learning."

In developing her theory, Dweck undertook a series of studies beginning in the late 1970s with a look at 130 fifth-graders attending schools in semirural communities near Urbana-Champaign, Illinois. She and clinical psychologist Carol Diener, PhD, divided them into two groups—"helpless" and "mastery"—based on their performance on an intellectual achievement responsibility scale.

The children tackled a series of unsolvable problems while Dweck and Diener recorded their comments. Although both groups performed equally well, they reacted differently to their mistakes.

"The helpless kids quickly gave up and decided they had failed, often blaming their own inability," said Diener, who teaches at the University of Illinois. "Mastery kids focused on how to do better in the future."

Helpless children downplayed their success at solving previous problems and held little hope of success, while mastery children remembered previous victories and felt confident that they'd figure out other problems. They said things like "I did it before, I can do it again," or "I like puzzles," while their less confident peers said things like "I'm not smart enough," or "I want to quit doing this."

Dweck replicated these results in other samples throughout the 1980s, as she built her theory that children's perceptions affect their learning.

A Fall From Smarts

Despite their different reactions to failure, incremental and entity theorists' academic performance is similar during elementary school, Dweck found. Not until junior high, when academic demands heighten, do the groups start to pull apart.

Often children who do best in elementary school are most vulnerable in junior high because they may be used to easy successes and know so little of failure, Dweck noted.

"Entity theory manifests itself in the face of challenge and failure," said Dweck. "If life were one big grade school, you probably wouldn't see these vulnerabilities emerging."

In 1990, she and colleague Valanne MacGyvers, PhD, now at the University of Southwestern Louisiana, tracked the impact of achievement on the motivational patterns of 226 seventh-graders at several challenging junior high schools also near Urbana-Champaign. They classified children according to entity or incremental theorizing and high or low confidence. The distribution was roughly equal across groups.

Based on students' grades and achievement-test scores, the researchers found that incremental theorists earned better grades than would be predicted. Those who had been high achievers in sixth-grade remained high achievers, and those who were low-achievers in sixth-grade improved significantly in seventh-grade. Even former low-achievers with low confidence improved dramatically—some of them earning the highest grades.

Stark differences to these patterns emerged for entity theorists. Low confidence, low-achievers remained so, and many former highly confident high-achievers became the lowest achievers in seventh grade. In fact, their achievement plummeted more than any other group's.

These ex-star students, often girls, fall prey to a naive adolescent belief that those who have to work hard are stupid, Dweck said. Earlier overconfidence in their abilities also hurts them. Teachers and parents often shower praise on these children in the easier elementary years, which appears to only reinforce their belief that smartness comes without effort.

While Dweck concedes that natural giftedness helps, she believes that motivation and *perception* of ability are what really helps children realize their potential.

"Effort should be perceived as an ally, not a threat," said Dweck.

Learning Goals

A 1986 questionnaire survey of 133 eighth-graders by Dweck and colleague Ellen Leggett, PhD, confirmed that perception of effort, or hard work, makes all the difference. The survey participants were in the top two of four achievement tracks at Gibbs Junior High School in Arlington, Massachusetts. Students concerned with grades and test scores scorned effort even when it led to success, while those with learning goals saw them as a tool to understand material. Leggett, formerly an educational psychology professor at Harvard University and the University of California-Riverside, is now a litigation consultant in Los Angeles.

In keeping with Dweck's other studies, bright girls were more likely than bright boys to believe that making an effort meant they weren't smart. During the elementary years, boys more often misbehave, so teachers and parents scold them and make a concerted effort to instill work habits in them. Girls, however, are reinforced for their good behavior and "smartness," instead of developing a work ethic, said Leggett. Girls are also more likely to attribute a failure to their own inability, whereas boys are more likely to attribute it to lack of effort, said Leggett.

While entity beliefs may lead to diminished self-confidence in intelligence, they do not necessarily pull down girls' grades, Leggett noted. On paper they may do just as well as incremental theorists, but only because they probably avoid more challenging courses and subjects such as math and science.

Leggett blames society and school curricula for children's beliefs that intelligence is fixed.

"Children hear that Edison discovered electricity but they don't hear about his struggle to do it," said Leggett, "They don't hear that the process is just as important as the right answer, and that errors are a part of that process. Kids need to hear that the learning process is about exploring, taking risks, making mistakes, and learning a lot along the way."

Strong Emotions Can Blur the Source of a Memory

Beth Azar

The nation laughed when former-president Ronald Reagan confused movie scenes with real-life events. But life is full of such memory mistakes. And if no one is there to correct the source of our memory, we may go on believing something we saw in a movie, or even something we imagined actually happened.

Marcia Johnson, PhD, likes to talk about monitoring the source of our memories to distinguish between memory and reality. Is it from a newspaper? The radio? Did someone tell you? Was it something you experienced? Or was it something you imagined or dreamed? To separate reality from fiction, people must answer these kinds of questions.

But remembering the source of a memory isn't always easy, said Johnson. People remember memories as real or imagined based on various characteristics of the memory.

Memories derived from perception—things you read, see, experience—tend to have more perceptual detail than memories derived from imagination, which have more information about thoughts and feelings. So if an activated memory has a lot of perceptual detail —"I remember the color of the book and the look of the page"—but not a lot of information about thoughts, a person will most likely conclude it's a perceptual, not imagined memory.

People can also retrieve additional information to support or reject the source of a particular memory. For example, is the memory plausible given other knowledge one has? If you remember a colleague chewing out your boss at a staff meeting, but other knowledge places him in the hospital at the time of the meeting, you'd have to reject the memory as mere fantasy.

From the *APA Monitor*, October 1995, p. 31.

In her studies, Johnson manipulates subjects' perceptions and imaginations, then examines how accurately they can name the source of their memories. She's found that how a person remembers something—whether through perceptual details or by remembering emotions—strongly predicts how well they can name the memory source.

Perception and Processing

Johnson has found that the more memories from imagination are like perceptions, the more subjects will confuse imagination with perception.

In one study, Johnson showed pictures to subjects two, five, or eight times. Between presentation trials, subjects were asked to imagine the pictures. Researchers then asked subjects to remember how often they had seen the various pictures, ignoring the times they imagined them.

"The more times subjects imagined a picture, the more times they think they saw it," said Johnson.

But it's not just perceptual qualities that matter, it's also how the information is processed, she said. In another study, she manipulated how subjects processed items to see how it would affect how they remembered details later. She showed them a series of items presented as words or line drawings, varying how subjects processed the items.

One group had to indicate the function of the item — "knife," for example, would be used to cut. Such a task doesn't *require* a person to use imagery although they might spontaneously. One group had to indicate a relevant feature—a knife has a blade. This task also doesn't require imagery. The third group had to rate how long it would have taken an artist to draw a line drawing of the item. This task requires explicit imagery.

Afterwards subjects took a surprise test that asked them to indicate whether an object appeared as a word, as a picture, or did not appear at all. Subjects who processed the objects by rating how long an artist would take to draw it rarely claimed to have seen an object when they actually saw a word. Subjects in the other two groups had a harder time remembering whether they'd seen a picture or a word.

"These studies illustrate that both perceptual quality and cognitive operations are important cues for reality monitoring," said Johnson.

Emotions Get in the Way

Johnson conducted another series of studies examining memories of experiences. She found that emotions can blur the source of memories by decreasing the amount of perceptual information available.

Subjects who think about their thoughts and feelings during the event—whether imagined or real—remember fewer perceptual aspects of the event than subjects who think about the perceptual details of the event, such as colors or spatial locations of objects. These subjects also rated perceived and imagined events as more alike than subjects who thought about perceptual qualities.

In other studies, Johnson found that older subjects (aged 60 years or more) remember more thoughts and emotions just after a real or imagined event than younger subjects (aged 17 to 30). Also, when asked to recall whether the event was real or imagined three weeks later, older subjects were wrong significantly more often than younger subjects.

To examine this phenomenon further, she devised a study to simulate an autobiographical experience. Pairs of subjects played roles in a short play: Two roommates meet on a subway platform, ride home together, and on arriving home confront a problem with the electricity. The experimenter gives the subjects their lines and says whether or not a line should be said aloud. The "actors"—young and older adults—say or think the lines as indicated.

After performing the play, the experimenter put subjects in three groups: (a) The perceptual focus group tried to remember what was said during the play, (b) the affective focus group tried to remember what they felt during the play, and (c) the control group tried to recall anything they could without any particular focus.

The experimenter then gave all subjects a surprise written test. Giving statements presented in random order, subjects had to indicate whether or not a statement was from the script, whose line it was, and whether it was said aloud or simply thought.

Younger subjects scored about the same regardless of the group they were in. But for older subjects, instructions on how to think about the play seemed to make a big difference in source monitoring. Older subjects in the control group did much worse than younger subjects in being able to discriminate what they said from what the other person said. Scores stayed about the same for older subjects in the affective focus group. However, those in the perceptual focus group scored as high as younger subjects.

"One reason older adults have more difficulty in source monitoring situations is that they may be more likely to focus on affective qualities of experience," said Johnson. "This may be at the expense of perceptual aspects of experience."

These results "suggest the possibility that those ideas we have strong [emotional] responses to may be the ones we're least likely to be able to identify the origins of later," said Johnson.

"Imagined events as well as actual events can be promoted to rich autobiographical status," concluded Johnson. "Focusing on the emotional qualities during an event or when you think about it later sometimes may have a negative impact on source monitoring."

The consequences? "We may be haunted by traumas in childhood that never took place or deny those that did, testify to events that never happened, cut off a friendship over words that were never said."

3

Motivation and Emotion

Top Athletes Focus on Tasks, Not Trophies

Beth Azar

Motivational sport psychologists don't want to take the thrill out of victory, but they would like to take the agony out of defeat.

They've been developing a theory of motivation and achievement over the past two decades. And they're finding that the traditional winner-takes-all philosophy so prevalent in sports does little to encourage athletic performance.

Instead, focusing on incremental improvement and mastering a task best predicts achievement, enjoyment, and staying power for elite and recreational athletes alike.

The Motivational Climate

The sports motivation theory grew directly out of an academic motivation theory developed in the early 1980s by a group of University of Illinois researchers, including John Nicholls, PhD, Martin Maehr, PhD, (now at the University of Michigan) and Carol Dweck, PhD (now at Columbia University).

Glyn Roberts, PhD, who helped develop the motivation theory as it applies to sports, has spent the last 25 years studying elite athletes and children in competitive environments.

The basic theory states that motivation to achieve depends on two primary types of goals. Ego-oriented goals produce the win-motivated style, and task-oriented goals produce the task-mastery style. (The terminology differs somewhat depending on the researcher.) Most sports researchers believe people can be highly or slightly oriented toward

From the *APA Monitor*, July 1996, p. 21.

either or both types of goals. The combination of the two helps predict achievement.

A person's goal orientation can be altered by the climate they operate in, said sport psychologist Joan L. Duda, PhD, of Purdue University. So if teachers, parents, or coaches emphasize ego goals over task goals, students, children, and athletes will likely hold ego-oriented goals.

Duda has found several factors that lay the bases for an ego-focused climate:

- Athletes believe the coach will harshly evaluate mistakes.
- The coaches give most of the attention and recognition to star players.
- The coaches not only emphasize beating a competitor but also create a rivalry among their own players, pitting them against each other.

In a task-oriented training climate, coaches

- reinforce effort and execution above outcome;
- encourage athletes to challenge themselves to improve their technique; and
- convey that everyone has an equal role to play, even though they recognize ability differences among the players.

"In a task-oriented climate coaches and players focus on the process rather than the product," added sport psychologist Darren Treasure, PhD, of Southern Illinois University at Edwardsville.

Ego Versus Task

The academic research clearly demonstrates that highly task-oriented people enjoy learning more, stick with school longer, and perform better than ego-oriented people. And there's even evidence that ego-orientation hinders success in school, especially if a child begins to doubt his or her ability.

Roberts and Treasure find the same trend for children involved in sports—they're better off if they're motivated by mastering skills and trying their best than if they're motivated by winning.

Before age 12, all children are generally task focused, said Roberts. Young children don't recognize the difference between effort and ability and believe that trying hard equals success. By age 12 they begin to recognize that effort doesn't always equal ability. And if they're in an ego-focused environment they begin to define success as beating others.

"Then, if they don't win they drop out," said Roberts.

From ages 12 and 17, 90% of children drop out of sports programs, he explained. He believes the trend is fueled by coaches and parents who promote an ego focus and de-emphasize a task focus.

If coaches switch from primarily ego-focused coaching to primarily task-focused coaching, children enjoy the sport more, extract more satisfaction from their play, want to practice more, and view sports more as a lifelong activity than as a mechanism to enhance their status among their peers, Roberts found.

Duda's research with recreational and elite athletes finds that those who rely on ego goals, with little concern for task goals, are emotionally fragile. They have a hard time handling a slump, an injury, or a drop in rank.

"They don't have enough of a task focus to sustain the quality of the experience," said Duda.

"If a fear of losing dominates an athlete's thinking, he will experience a lot of stress and disappointment," said psychologist Robert Singer, PhD, of the University of Miami.

"But if he measures success by the scale of 'Am I getting better?' he'll see self-improvement, he'll be happier, and will persist longer." But an ego orientation might not be all bad, at least not for elite athletes, said Roberts. He and others find that those athletes who make it into the elite ranks rate high on both ego- and task-goal orientations.

They can switch back and forth between the two depending on the context, said Roberts. They use an ego orientation in competition when winning is the most important thing. But when they need to put time into practice, they switch to a task orientation. This is important because task-oriented people like to practice, but ego-oriented people hate it, said Roberts.

Duda adds that while an ego focus can provide an extra kick toward winning during competition, even then a task focus is important to help athletes maintain their focus on the moment.

For elite athletes "the trick is finding the right balance between the two," Roberts added.

Research Plumbs Why the "Talking Cure" Works

Beth Azar

Cognitive therapy, group therapy, behavioral therapy, psychoanalysis—they all work to help people deal with emotional stress. But why do they all work? One common denominator is disclosure: the telling of one's story.

It's widely known that keeping problems bottled up inside can cause emotional and physical stress. But when and how people disclose their problems can be just as significant as whether they disclose at all, according to an international group of researchers.

Therapies in which people disclose their problems "bring about change because having people tell their story brings about change," said psychologist James Pennebaker, PhD, of Southern Methodist University in Dallas.

What Are You Feeling?

Telling one's story means more than simply relating the facts of an event. Bernard Rimé, PhD, of the Catholic University of Louvain in Louvain-La-Neuve, Belgium, provides data on the critical importance of sharing emotions as opposed to sharing only facts. In one study, he and his colleagues interviewed women the day after they had given birth. They asked one set of women detailed questions about their emotional state during delivery and another set about their pregnancy and their daily lives. Six weeks after the interview, women who had been asked about their emotional state experienced fewer unpleasant memories of

From the *APA Monitor*, November 1994, p. 24.

delivery and recovered better than those who did not share their emotions, Rimé found.

Active nondisclosure poses its own problems, separate from simple nondisclosure, according to psychologist Dan Wegner, PhD, of the University of Virginia. Actively suppressed thoughts bubble up to form intrusive, preoccupying thoughts about the very thing people are trying to suppress.

Keeping thoughts secret creates a suppression cycle: The thought immediately comes to mind, the person tries to suppress it again, and the cycle continues. Wegner hypothesizes that disclosing suppressed thoughts may stop this cycle and prevent intrusive thoughts.

Nondisclosure may be more than just intrusive. Suppressed expressions may have medical as well as psychological implications, according to research by Harald Traue, PhD, of the department of medical psychology at Universitat Ulm in Ulm, Germany. His work links headaches to scant facial expression and back pain to decreased expressive behavior and increased muscle activity. Traue concluded that "inhibited expressiveness should not be seen as a symptom but looked upon as a 'risk factor' in the etiology of back pain."

The Mind–Body Connection

It's not just muscle aches and head pains that nondisclosure affects. Psychological stress may also affect the immune system, which guards people against disease, according to Keith Petrie, PhD, of the department of psychiatry and behavioral science at the University of Auckland Medical School, New Zealand.

"There is considerable data now to suggest that when individuals actively inhibit emotional expression, they show measurable immunological changes consistent with poorer health outcomes," wrote Petrie and his colleagues in a summary of the research in this area.

He and colleagues recently examined immune responses to a Hepatitis B vaccine using a writing paradigm designed by Pennebaker. The paradigm randomly assigns subjects to an emotional or a control writing group. Researchers instruct those in the emotional writing group to write about traumatic experiences and focus on emotional issues that they may not have expressed before. The control group is asked to write about trivial things.

Petrie's group asked subjects to write about their assigned topics for 20 minutes per day for four days immediately prior to receiving a Hepatitis B vaccine.

"Compared with the control group, subjects in the emotional expression group showed significantly higher antibody levels against hepatitis B over the subsequent six-month period," said Petrie. Such results imply a stronger immune response for subjects who expressed their emotions.

The Dangers of Disclosure

Without a receptive audience, however, people disclosing their troubles may be worse off than if they'd never confessed, according to Roxane Cohen Silver, PhD, based on her research from the program in social ecology at the University of California, Irvine.

In one study, Silver interviewed a group of 1,126 Vietnam veterans. She found that, in general, the more a veteran talked about his experience postwar, the less distress and reflection he experienced now. However, veterans who reported that people did not want to hear about what happened to them in Vietnam experienced more distress, reflection, intrusive thoughts, and avoidant thoughts than veterans who received support from those they spoke to.

Silver found similar results for parents who had lost an infant to sudden infant death syndrome and people in California who had lost homes to fire.

Do Roots of Violence Grow From Nature or Nurture?

Beth Azar and Scott Sleek

In the autobiography he wrote from his prison cell, Los Angeles gang member Monster Kody Scott—who shot his first victim at age 11 and is now serving time for robbery—blames his problems on his parent's destitution and violent fights. So what about Scott's three brothers and two sisters?

Although they all grew up in the same environment, only one brother is a gang member. The rest lead productive, law-abiding lives. In fact, an older sister is in the Air Force while another sister is studying data processing. An older brother is an actor.

Psychologist David Rowe, PhD, of the University of Arizona, uses Scott's family as an example to illustrate his contention that genes play a larger role than family influence in children's personality traits. Yet others, like Gerald R. Patterson, PhD, of the Oregon Social Learning Center, Eugene, Oregon, believe the family environment is the predominant personality molder.

Environment

Patterson pieced together what's known about aggression in children and adults to form a developmental theory of aggression and violence based on family and peer influence.

Aggressive and antisocial children seem to move through stages, said Patterson. As preschoolers, they form oppositional defiant personalities—throwing temper tantrums and acting coercive and defiant. They move on to develop conduct disorders, such as fighting,

From the *APA Monitor*, October 1994, p. 31.

stealing, and drug-taking, which can lead to early arrest, chronic delinquency, and violence.

Not all children at the beginning of this cycle will end up at the end of the cycle, said Patterson. However, most who get to the end of the cycle will have gone through each stage.

Children learn conflict-coping skills from their families. Coercive children appear to come from families that display five times the conflict of families of non-coercive children, Patterson said.

Patterson doesn't rule out biological factors, but "thinks it's a combination of a difficult-to-train infant and socially unskilled parents that provides the mix that gets this whole thing going."

Normal children cope with conflict by using prosocial skills— talking, humor, sidetracking, and deflecting—and coercive tactics—temper tantrums, hitting, and noncompliance. Both methods work equally well, but the prosocial skills are better accepted by the family.

Problem children learn that coercive skills alone work in their already conflict-ridden home. The child winds up unskilled at prosocial skills and very likely to respond coercively in a wide variety of situations.

When these antisocial, coercive children enter school, there is a predictable impact on the social environment:

- They are rejected by their peers within a few hours.
- They spend less and less time doing work.
- They perform poorly on academic tests and on IQ tests.
- They become sad, miserable, and often depressed.

These children are now set up all too well to enter the deviant peer group—the second source of reinforcement for their behavior.

What this means for treatment and prevention is that "if you want to be effective you need to get started with families before [the children] go through the cascade of effect," said Patterson. "It's almost too late by the age of 8 or 9."

As children age, the peer group's influence outstrips that of the family. Research has found that deviant kids hang out with deviant kids and that they "mutually reinforce each other" through rule-breaking language, body postures, and antisocial attitudes, said Patterson.

He has also found that there are two types of delinquent kids: "early starters" who get arrested for the first time before age 14, and "late starters" who get arrested for the first time between age 14 and 16. Studies show that as many as 75% of chronic offenders are early starters. The earlier the first arrest, the more likely a kid will be arrested again within three years.

"There's a transitive progression going from the antisocial trait score to early onset, chronicity, and to violence," said Patterson.

Genes

Rowe, author of the book *The Limits of Family Influence*, believes child development experts focus too much on environmental influences—such as the parents' childrearing techniques—and not enough on genetics. Shared traits between a parent and child are also more closely connected to genetic heredity than to a child's mimicry, he said. A child's genotype shapes what he or she acquires through various life experiences, he said.

"At parental urging, a shy child can be taught to speak effectively in front of his sixth grade classmates," Rowe explained. "But the child stays basically shy. Before a different group, he feels anxious and worried again."

"The shy child is less likely to become a politician than the bold one. The bold child is less likely to become a computer programmer than the shy one. Children gravitate toward many different experiences, but choose to stay with those that reinforce their genetic dispositions," Rowe said.

A well-known Minnesota study of twins separated and raised apart showed family nurturing contributed only slightly to each twin's personality development, Rowe noted. Other studies show the compared IQs of siblings raised apart were similar to those raised together, bolstering Rowe's belief that family experiences don't influence a child's intellectual capability.

In the environmental area, Rowe, along with Joseph Lee Rodgers, PhD, of the University of Oklahoma, contend that non-shared social influences—experiences that are unique to each child in a family setting—have a larger sway on one's behavior than shared influences. Non-shared influences account for the unique traits of each child within a family, Rodgers said. Thus, a girl's personality emanates more from her peer relationships, and the way her parents treat her compared to her brother, than from the upbringing she and her brother share, he contends.

The number of times a mother spanks one son compared to the other, or the amount of time a father spends reading to a daughter compared to a son, may constitute non-shared influences.

"What parents do to treat their children differently is probably at least as important as what they do to account for their similarities," he said.

Rodgers and others are conducting ongoing research into how adolescents' non-shared experiences correlate with the age in which they started having sex and their propensity for delinquency. Under the project, researchers began annual interviews in 1979 with 12,000 adolescents—many of them within the same families—who were then aged 14 to 21. Subjects are asked each year about their economic status, fertility history, marital status, education, and other measures. Researchers also inquired about their first sexual intercourse and their past delinquent behavior.

So far, the data indicate that the age at which the subjects' lose their virginity hinges mainly on their non-shared influences, he said.

The findings could sway future social policy, Rodgers said. Parents and teachers may have to consider alternatives to "one-size-fits-all" education and nurturing. "You don't design parenting styles and school programs that are being consumed equally by all kids," Rodgers said.

4 Cognition

Attitude Affects Memory, Decisions, and Performance

Beth Azar

Do you accentuate the positive or just try to avoid the negative? You probably do both depending on the situation, but most people lean toward one or the other. And those personal leanings help shape how they make decisions and approach problems, according to psychologist E. Tory Higgins, PhD, of Columbia University.

Traditional models of motivation revolve around pain and pleasure. People stop doing what's painful and continue doing what's pleasurable. Higgins proposes adding a second dimension to this model called "regulatory focus."

Two Focuses

He's found two types of regulatory focus: People who are "promotion-focused" view pain and pleasure in terms of the absence or presence of positives and try to promote positives. People who are "prevention-focused" view pain and pleasure in terms of the presence or absence of negatives and try to prevent negatives (see Figure 1).

The two types of focus are based on our evolutionary need for nurture and security, suggested Higgins. Nurture fosters a promotion focus, emphasizing the potential positives of life. Security fosters a prevention focus, emphasizing the potential negatives and a need to avoid them.

People can use both focus systems, but some people, known as "chronics," use one focus system predominantly. According to research by Higgins and his colleagues, either focus can affect what people re-

From the *APA Monitor*, November 1995, p. 27.

Figure 1

	Pain (negatives)	Pleasure (positives)	
Promotion focused	**Absence of positives**	**Presence of positives**	Strategy → Promote Positives
Prevention focused	**Presence of negatives**	**Absence of negatives**	Strategy → Prevent Negatives

A four-pronged model of motivation.

member about events, how they perform certain tasks, and how they regulate their emotions.

Higgins found that people remember aspects of events that match their regulatory focus. For example, a promotion-focused person better remembers the details of a story about a man finding a $20 bill (presence of positive) than a story about getting stuck on a subway (presence of negative). For a prevention-focused person, memory is better for getting stuck on a subway.

When he has induced people to have a particular focus in a given situation, he has found the same effect on memory. In one study, he falsely told subjects he was testing the influence of exercise on physiology by collecting hormones from their saliva while they performed different exercises.

Subjects rode an exercise bike with a cotton ball in their mouth that tasted either bitter or sweet. This promoted the pain or pleasure dimension. Next subjects performed a mental exercise with a new cotton ball in their mouth and read four stories like the ones in his first study that represented the absence or presence of positive or the absence or presence of negative. The new cotton ball tasted neutral or maintained the taste they had before. This promoted a person's regulatory focus: Subjects experienced either sweet–sweet (presence of positive), sweet–neutral (absence of positive), bitter–bitter (presence of negative) or bitter–neutral (absence of negative).

Subjects then took a memory test about the stories. Higgins again found that subjects with an induced promotion focus—sweet–sweet and sweet–neutral—remembered the presence and absence of positive events better than the presence and absence of negative events. The opposite was true for the prevention-focused subjects—bitter–bitter, bitter–neutral. How people approach a goal or problem affects the strategies they use, according to other studies by Higgins. He asserts there are two basic strategies to problem-solving: approaching matches by seeing everything as an opportunity, and avoiding mismatches by seeing everything as a potential hazard.

To test whether focus affects strategy, Higgins induced focus in a group of subjects who thought they were participating in a simple skills-test experiment. From a questionnaire given two months before the experiment, he selected two activities for each subject, one they liked and one they disliked. He told each subject they'd be doing two tasks, a memory recognition task and one of two other activities—the one they liked, such as playing a game similar to the game show *Jeopardy*, or the one they disliked, such as proofreading.

Higgins formed five groups by putting five different contingencies on the memory recognition task: (a) Controls—randomly chose which of the two alternate activities they did; (b) presence of positive—if they did well on the recognition task, they would play *Jeopardy* instead of proofread; (c) absence of positive—if they didn't do well on the memory task, they would not get to play *Jeopardy*, and would have to proofread; (d) absence of negative—if they didn't do poorly, they wouldn't have to proofread, they would get to play *Jeopardy*; and (e) presence of negative—if they did poorly, they would have to proofread instead of play *Jeopardy*.

Everyone's goal, Higgins assumed, was do the task they liked. The strategies, however, would vary depending on the focus; they would either try to do well on the memory recognition task or try to avoid doing poorly. In the memory recognition task, subjects saw a sequence of nonsense words. They then saw another list and had to say whether a nonsense word was from the first list or not. He found that the promotion-focused subjects—the presence and absence of positive groups—tended to say "yes" to every word. The prevention-focused people, tended to say "no" to every word. This makes sense, said Higgins, because promotion-focused people want correct answers, and the best way to get them is to look for word matches: They seek out more opportunities to find them. But for prevention-focused people, every opportunity is a chance to be wrong, which they want to avoid. So they avoid word mismatches by saying no to everything.

Using Both Strategies

Focus not only affects memory and strategies, it affects outlook and emotions, said Higgins. He's found that promotion-focused people feel happy and satisfied when they see their lives are going well, and sad and disappointed during times of trouble. Prevention-focused people feel secure and calm when they see their lives as not going badly, and nervous and tense during adverse times.

For people who regularly use both systems, emotions crop up depending on the system they're using at the time. For example, when people are sad, the promotion system isn't working. But it might be good for it to shut down, as it forces people to rethink their goals, Higgins said.

When prevention isn't working and fear sets in, it may mean the person has something legitimate to fear. But "when people get stuck at the extremes, people can get very depressed or anxious," said Higgins. Learning more about these regulatory systems could help psychologists better understand how people regulate their lives, he said.

Psychologists Question Findings of *Bell Curve*

Tori DeAngelis

Although the authors of *The Bell Curve* assert that low-IQ, minority women who have multiple children are helping to "dumb down" America, several data-based arguments counter that line of thinking, said Stephen Ceci, PhD, a cognitive psychologist at Cornell University. Ceci reported findings from an American Psychological Association (APA) task force on intelligence and *The Bell Curve* created in response to the controversial book.

One finding is that Blacks as a group are catching up to Whites' IQ levels, Ceci said. Data from the respected National Educational Longitudinal Surveys, for instance, show that the verbal achievement for Black and White 13- to 17-year-olds closed considerably between the early 1970s and 1990. "We're getting a convergence, not a divergence," he said.

The APA task force sought to address what is known about intelligence and to develop a report on the topic.[1] The group studied the science and politics of the book "in an unbiased, systematic manner," according to Ulric Neisser, PhD, of Emory University and task force chair. It examined issues including the link between genes and intelligence, the impact of environment on intelligence, and individual differences in intelligence.

The task force members contended that although some of the book's data are strong, they are being used for a dubious political agenda. And some of the data are off-base, they said.

From the *APA Monitor*, October 1995, p. 7.
[1]The report appeared in the February 1996 issue of the *American Psychologist*.

The Controversy

Written by Richard Herrnstein, PhD, the late Harvard psychologist, and Charles Murray, PhD, of the American Enterprise Institute, *The Bell Curve* concludes that there are large individual differences in intelligence, that those differences are to a large extent inherited, and that they are related to important differences in real-world outcomes, such as how much money a person earns.

While many books and research papers have been written to justify those claims, Ceci maintained that despite their agenda, Herrnstein and Murray are "the clearest and most comprehensive writers" on the topic to date.

Many of the book's data are accurate, Ceci believes. He agrees, for instance, with the authors' contention that intelligence is correlated with factors such as schooling, welfare dependency, and job performance.

But other arguments and conclusions in the book Ceci found simply wrong, both in data and interpretation, he said. In particular, he strongly disagrees with the authors' conclusion that "genetic forces are exerting a downward pressure on the cognitive capital in the United States," he said.

The Bell Curve authors contend that the gene pool for intelligence is diminished when young, low-IQ women have babies. More young, minority women with low IQs have babies than White women. So for every three generations of high-IQ people, for example, there might be four generations of low-IQ people, the two argue.

One way to test whether such a social force is diminishing the collective American IQ is to ask whether the IQs of children of wealthy parents and those of poor people are getting farther apart over time, Ceci said. In fact, intelligence-test data from the 1930s to 1989 show that they're growing closer together. For instance, the IQ gap between those at the top and bottom rungs of the social hierarchy in job status has shrunk from a 12.5-point difference in the 1930s to an 8.5-point difference today, with people testing higher on average than they used to, he said.

Several environmental factors suggest reasons why, Ceci said. In that time period, classrooms were desegregated under federal law; income rose slightly for Blacks but not for Whites; and more Blacks graduated from college, he noted.

The Bell Curve also propounds several notions that are actually myths, each of which can be debunked by more reasoned explanations and data, said Robert Sternberg, PhD, of Yale University. Each myth likewise has a prevailing countermyth that is equally false, he added.

For example, the book argues that intelligence is a single entity. The countermyth is that "intelligence is so many things that you can hardly count them," Sternberg said.

The intermediate and more truthful position is that "there is a psychometric of general ability, but there's more to intelligence than 'g,'"—the traditional measure of global intelligence, Sternberg said. Research with students in his Yale laboratory, for instance, shows that testing students for creative, synthetic, and practical aptitudes as well as analytical ability illuminates a broader range of skills than IQ tests do.

Another nonfactual myth propounded by Herrnstein and Murray is that "the social order is a natural outcome of the IQ pecking order," Sternberg said. The countermyth is that "IQ doesn't matter at all."

It's instructive to imagine what would happen if society used other kinds of tests besides those of intelligence to determine class status—such as height, Sternberg said. In that scheme, Harvard Law School would admit only students taller than 6′4″, Yale Law School only students 6′3″ and taller, and so on. Consequently, becoming a lawyer would be contingent on your height.

Genes and Intelligence

Thomas Bouchard, PhD, a researcher at the University of Minnesota, agreed with the book's contention that intelligence has a sizable genetic component. One line of research suggests that as people age, the effects of heredity on intelligence rise as those of the environment fall, Bouchard said. Thus, as people grow older and interact more with their environments, their genetic potential becomes more evident. No matter what a person's initial upbringing, for instance, someone with superior intelligence will find ways to use their intelligence in the environment, while a less intelligent person will not be able to manipulate the environment as capably. Additional research shows that unrelated people who are raised together in childhood share many characteristics in common at first, but lose them as they move into adulthood, he said.

John Loehlin, PhD, of the University of Texas at Austin, argued that people have misinterpreted the authors' points. While Herrnstein and Murray do argue that genes play a role in the heritability of intelligence, they also think environment can be implicated, he said.

To *The Bell Curve* authors, the effect matters more than the cause: "Who has the babies and how early they have them affects the characteristics of the next generation in either case," Loehlin said.

A "Gloomy Vision"

Ellin Bloch, PhD, of the California School of Professional Psychology, offered an impassioned argument against the book.

"There is a kind of superficial, melancholy tone to this book, underneath which lies a gloomy vision of America and its people in relation to one another," she said.

Bloch asserted that the book sets forth "a scientific determinism or fatalism" in which a cognitive elite stays on top, while less intelligent citizens take appointed places on lower social rungs.

It's dangerous to mix this incendiary position with politics, Bloch believes. Such a view is "profoundly antipsychological and antidemocrative in nature, and it engenders a social politics without sympathy."

Nathan Brody, PhD, of Wesleyan University, said that while the authors' descriptions concerning variance in intelligence may be true, they provide no socially enlightening antidote for the problem. What's important, he believes, is how society responds to those differences.

"We have to think about the environment and what it provides," Brody said. "How can we intervene to help people who are not using what's provided in an optimal way? We need to learn a lot more about the interface between aptitudes and the way we structure our environment to help people develop their abilities."

Breaking Through Barriers to Creativity

Beth Azar

Mr. Speer was killed one evening in 1835 when the axle on the rail car he controlled broke. The accident threw him from his seat atop the rail car, which crushed him as it overturned.

Speer's untimely death—and those of many conductors of the time—occurred because the first train designers couldn't see beyond standard vehicle designs. Early train cars required conductors to ride on top of the car like stage coach drivers: The invention that came first—the stage coach—limited the designers' creativity.

Most innovators base their work on prior knowledge and experience, a reliance that can help or hinder the creative process. Cognitive psychologists are finding that people may have little control over the past's influence. Who we are, what we know, and what we've already experienced thrusts itself into the creative process, providing both structure and obstruction.

Limits on Imagination

Certain properties make objects, people, and even ideas what they are. A dog, for example, has four legs, a tail, fur, and it barks. When you see a dog, no matter what shape, you can tell it's a dog and not a bird or a cat. Psychologists call these central properties because they're key to identifying a concept.

But central properties also limit imagination. Research conducted by Thomas Ward, PhD, of Texas A&M University shows that when asked to draw imaginary animals, subjects tend to draw creatures with the

From the *APA Monitor*, August 1995, pp. 1, 20.

central properties of conventional animals: symmetrical with two or four legs, eyes, and a distinct head.

Even children, who some argue are freer from creative constraint, give imaginary animals features similar to those of existing animals, according to a recent study by Cristina Cacciari, PhD, of the University of Bologna, Italy.

She asked a group of 37 preschoolers and 38 fifth graders to draw imaginary houses and animals. Although the drawings showed creativity, none went beyond the common structures of real houses and animals. Houses had roofs, chimneys, windows, and doors, while animals had appendages, eyes, mouths, noses, and ears.

Not surprisingly, recent events cloud creativity more than past events. Ward and his colleagues Steven Smith, PhD, and Jay Shumacher, PhD, showed subjects examples of imaginary animals with four legs, tails, and a head. When they asked them to draw their own imaginary animals, as different from the examples as possible, people nevertheless drew animals with four legs, a head, and a tail.

"We tend to view examples as positive things, but they can be bad if they restrict the range of options available," said Ward.

Being Human

In part, our very existence limits how far we can take our imaginations, according to research by Raymond Gibbs, PhD, of the University of California, Santa Cruz. Humans exist inside bodies that feel the effects of gravity and biochemical processes. They interact with the environment and with each other in relatively static ways.

These natural limits resonate in the way people use and understand language, says Gibbs. From bodily experiences such as standing, walking, eating, and interacting with the physical environment, people develop mental models—what Gibbs calls image schemas—of concepts such as balance, containment, resistance, and verticality.

These same concepts crop up in language. For example, another image schema is "source-path-goal." Humans often move along a path to reach a goal—across the room to get a book, down the road to see a friend. People recognize abstract concepts, such as "life is a journey" and sayings such as, "we're at the crossroads," and "we've gotten off the track" because they have an innate understanding of the source-path-goal theme, says Gibbs.

People also use the image schemas to form and understand multiple meanings for the same word. *Stand*, for example, can be used in the physical sense to say "the lamp stands on the table," or in the abstract sense to say "he took a stand on the issue."

"People recognize connections between various bodily experiences and different aspects of linguistic meaning," said Gibbs.

To test this theory, Gibbs had people judge how relevant the various image schemas are to the concept of physically standing. He found that people relate ideas of resistance, verticality, and balance to standing, but not ideas such as source-path-goal or containment.

Gibbs had people rate how relevant those schemas are to different uses of the word "stand." He found that each use is characterized by a pattern of relevant image schemas. For example, with the phrase "to stand against great odds," people bring up images of resistance but not of verticality. With the statement "the clock stands on the mantle," people bring up images of balance and verticality more than resistance.

Image schemas allow people to progress from real, bodily experiences to more abstract concepts. From thinking of the body as a container that substances enter and exit, people can think of themselves or other objects being inside other containers such as houses or cars. From there, people can think of being "in love." "They're in the love container," said Gibbs. "They can fall into it and get dumped out of it."

Gibbs also examined phrases people use to describe physical states. People say "he blew his stack," "he hit the roof," or "it made my blood boil," when describing anger. When Gibbs asked people to form a mental image of these phrases, he consistently got descriptions of containers under great pressure with a boiling or hot fluid that escapes violently.

"We're constrained by our embodied experience," said Gibbs. In one sense, such a constraint is limiting, but in another, it allows people to understand each other, even when they're being creative.

"It isn't as if creative geniuses—in say art or poetry—are thinking of entirely new concepts," he said. "They're making new twists on old concepts, which is why the reader can understand them, because they too have those embodied experiences."

Realizing the constraints on our creativity may help us avoid mistakes as glaring as the one that indirectly killed Mr. Speer. Ward and his colleagues are beginning work with engineers to see if they can foster innovation by teaching them how to think abstractly about problems.

For example, instead of thinking about a new brake system for cars based on improving one of the two existing brake systems, Ward suggests they think about the abstract design principles that a brake system must satisfy.

"Sometimes it's better and more efficient to start from what's been done before," said Ward. "But when you want innovation, it might be better to overcome the inertia pulling us toward the past."

5 Development

Adolescent Friends Not Always a Bad Influence

Hugh McIntosh

Early last year, a 14-year-old boy and his best friend planned and committed the murder of the boy's mother in a small Minnesota town.

Would the boy have killed his mother on his own? Perhaps not, suggests Willard Hartup, PhD, a University of Minnesota psychologist who studies peer relations in adulthood and early adolescence: "This murder was an unlikely event until these two antisocial friends reached consensus about it."

Only in the last decade have psychologists begun to explore the effects friendship have on adolescent development, the processes by which teens form friendships, and the factors that influence their relationships.

Research has led to some surprising findings: Teen "crowds" often ease the transition through adolescence, teens usually encourage each other in positive rather than negative ways, and parents may have far more sway with their adolescents than they realized.

Choosing Friends

Psychologists have long recognized that adolescents make friends with people who are similar to themselves. New research finds that teen cultures or crowds facilitate friend selection. According to psychologist Bradford Brown, PhD, of the University of Wisconsin at Madison,

From the *APA Monitor*, June 1996, p. 16.

crowds of "jocks," "druggies," "populars," "brains," "nerds," and "normals" channel adolescents toward particular relationships with peers.

"When kids choose a particular dress and grooming style, a set of activities on weekends, they're more or less placing themselves in a particular niche within the adolescent-peer social world that limits the kinds of relationships they're going to have with peers," Brown said.

Crowds engage adolescents at a time when they seek conformity. More important, these groups help adolescents develop identity and regulate social interactions.

Brown and his colleagues have also found that small groups of close friends wield more influence with adolescents than individual friends. In studies of adolescent peer groups of four or five, they found that clique characteristics predicted behavioral change in teens better than the qualities of the closest friend.

Influences of Peers

Peer influence can be positive or negative, but it's more likely to be the former than the latter, says psychologist Thomas Berndt, PhD, of Purdue University, who studies adolescent friendships and friends' influence.

Researchers have found, for example, that teens who did not smoke cigarettes reported their friends discouraged smoking, whereas children who smoked had friends whom they perceived as tolerating, rather than encouraging, smoking.

Berndt's own research on academic achievement showed that teens report their friends encourage them to do well in school instead of telling them not to worry about doing well.

But peer influence can be negative as well. As in the case of the mother's murder, teens are vulnerable to a "contagion effect," Berndt says. The theory holds that people in highly cohesive groups sometimes do things that they wouldn't do alone.

"The simple fact that the friend is there, even if the friend is not different in his attitudes from yours, makes antisocial acts more likely," Berndt said.

Research has also found that when deviant adolescents select deviant friends, their antisocial behaviors perpetuate in a downward spiral. In his studies of adolescents with high levels of alcohol and drug use, psychologist Michael Windle, PhD, of the Research Institute on Addiction in Buffalo, New York, found higher levels of arguments and other overt hostility among boys and more gossiping, rumor spreading, and other covert hostility among girls than in teen friendships not involving deviant behavior.

In a year-long study of friendships among deviant adolescents, Windle found that alcohol and drug abuse and delinquency became worse over time. He also found, however, that teens involved in delinquent behavior practiced a high degree of self-disclosure with their peers. Even though their friendships were more hostile and less reciprocal than average, these adolescents were looking for someone to talk with about their problems.

"Unfortunately, if they're in a highly deviant peer network, they're not likely to get a lot of constructive ideas of what they should do about their situation," Windle said.

Influence of Parents

Although teens might not like to admit it, parents can have an enormous influence on how they deal with friendships, experts say. An authoritative parenting style which combines control and warmth is particularly effective in moderating peer influence, says psychologist Nina Mounts, PhD, of the University of Illinois at Urbana-Champaign. Authoritative parents exercise a high degree of control but negotiate many of the particulars, such as curfew time.

In a study of ninth- through 11th-graders, Mounts and a colleague found that adolescents with authoritative parents were more strongly influenced by high-achieving friends and less influenced by drug-using friends than those with less authoritative parents.

Mounts also found that some parents directly influence their adolescents' friendships through management techniques, such as inviting over prosocial friends or advising teenagers not to hang out with certain friends. Her study found that teens whose parents used moderate amounts of management used drugs the least. Adolescents whose parents used higher or lower amounts had higher drug-use levels.

In addition, while friends influenced day-to-day issues, such as choice of clothes, parents influenced long-term issues such as educational choices.

It's difficult for parents to pick their teens' friends, said Brown. But they can help their children master the social skills needed for the new kinds of friendships formed at this age. And they can pick the environments from which their adolescents will select friends, if they have the foresight to nurture those environments in early childhood.

Schools the Source of Rough Transitions

Beth Azar

In September, thousands of 10- to 12-year-old children will face one of the most critical transitions of their lives—the move from elementary school to middle school. For some, it sparks a downward spiral that leads to school failure and withdrawal.

The switch from elementary school to junior high school coincides with several major changes for young adolescents. Most are in the throes of puberty; they're becoming more self-aware and self-conscious, and their thinking becomes more critical and complex. At the same time, parents and junior high teachers complain that the students are flagging both in motivation and performance.

Traditionally, parents, teachers, and even researchers blamed puberty alone for what they branded as inevitable declines in academic drive and achievement. But research psychologists are amassing evidence which shows the environment and philosophy of middle schools often conflict with the young adolescents' needs. Researchers are using developmental theories of motivation to explain this conflict and to show how children can avoid failure in middle school.

Developmental Mismatch

Since the early 1980s, psychologist Jacqueline Eccles, PhD, of the University of Michigan, and her colleagues, have collected data on the transition from elementary school to middle school. They've found that: (a) On average, children's grades drop dramatically during the first year of middle school, compared with grades in elementary school; (b) after

From the *APA Monitor*, June 1996, p. 14.

moving to junior high, children become less interested in school and less self-assured about their abilities; and (c) compared with elementary schools, middle schools are more controlling, less cognitively challenging, and focus more on competition and comparing students' ability.

The differences between elementary schools and middle schools cause what Eccles and her University of Michigan colleague Carol Midgely, PhD, call "developmental mismatch." They've found that middle school children report fewer opportunities for decision-making and lower levels of cognitive involvement than they had in elementary school, said Eccles' colleague, Eric Anderman, PhD, of the University of Kentucky.

At the same time, children must contend with a more complex social environment. They switch from a single teacher who knows their academic and social strengths to brief contact with many teachers. And they often face larger classes with a new group of peers.

These variables interact to make the transition to middle school challenging, said Anderman. Studies find that decreased motivation and self-assuredness contribute to poor academic performance. They have also found that drops in grades triggered by the transition can alter self-assuredness and motivation.

Goal Setting

To better explain how these environmental changes affect students, some researchers have turned to goal-orientation theory, developed by Carol Ames, PhD, and her colleagues at Michigan State University. The theory identifies two types of goals that motivate people to achieve in school.

Task goals encourage learning for learning's sake—people concentrate on mastering a task, rather than striving for an expected grade. Performance goals favor learning for performance's sake—people desire a good grade to prove their competence to others or to achieve a particular end, such as parental approval.

Everyone subscribes to both types of goals, said Midgely. We want to expand our knowledge base *and* get good grades. But most people lean more toward one than the other. Transition researchers speculate that elementary schools are more task-focused and middle schools are more performance-focused.

This shift may throw children off balance during the transition.

Indeed, several studies find that students become less task-oriented and more performance-oriented as they move from elementary school to middle school, and students believe their middle-school teachers focus more on performance than tasks. At the same time, their belief in their own academic ability decreases dramatically, the studies find.

A study by Anderman and Midgely found that grades decreased more for middle-school students who had been low achievers in elementary school than for those who had been high-achieving students at the elementary level. By the year after the transition, high achievers seemed to have bounced back from first year grade declines while low achievers failed to rebound.

"For the low achievers, the transition to the new environment sparks a downward spiral that they can't seem to recover from," said Anderman.

These longitudinal studies prove that changes in a child's goal orientation occur during the transition and these changes correlate with declines in motivation and performance, said Midgely. However, they don't prove that one causes the other. It's important to look beyond mean changes across big groups of students, she admits.

Carol Dweck, PhD, of Columbia University, agrees. She's found that some children thrive after the transition to middle school while others are particularly prone to failure.

The key is how they think about intelligence, she asserts. She found that children who think about intelligence as fixed—known as entity theorists—avoid tasks that challenge their ability or that risk failure. They instead choose to work on problems they know how to solve. Dweck calls this response pattern maladaptive or helpless. She believes it coincides with performance goals because the children prefer performing well to mastering something new.

Children who think about intelligence as malleable—known as incremental theorists—embrace challenging tasks and look at failure as a way to learn and improve. They tend to blame their failures on a lack of effort rather than a lack of ability. Dweck calls this response pattern mastery-oriented and believes it coincides with task goals.

Because elementary schools don't emphasize performance or failure versus success, the differences between the two types of theorists should not show up until after the transition to junior high school, said Dweck.

In a study of 165 seventh-grade students, one year after the transition to junior high, she found an overall decline in academic achievement, compared with achievement scores from sixth grade. But not all students' grades declined. Indeed, while confidence in one's ability seemed to predict grades in elementary school—high confidence children had the highest grades—intelligence theory took over in junior high. The grades of high-confidence incremental theorists stayed level but those of high-confidence entity theorists sank. Also, the grades of low-confidence incremental theorists soared while those of low-confidence entity theorists remained as low as in sixth grade.

"These high confidence kids who think intelligence is fixed, think that you should be able to do well without a lot of effort if you're smart," said Dweck. That strategy didn't work in the more-challenging middle school, where teachers judged performance not based on general knowledge but on task performance.

Meanwhile, the low-confidence incremental theorists blossomed in their new environment. They were more willing to face the challenge, said Dweck.

These studies imply that not all children will suffer a drop in academic performance when they enter middle school. However, both the school environment and children's goals and attitudes about learning and intelligence need to be re-evaluated, the researchers agree.

During the school-reform boom of the 1980s, middle schools were largely ignored, according to the final report of the Carnegie Council on Adolescent Development, released last year. That omission needs to be addressed and the research on adolescent motivation and school environment included in reform efforts, the report says.

Teens' Altruism Grows Like They Do—In Spurts

Nathan Seppa

As adolescents reach their late teens, they don't necessarily think more altruistically in making their moral judgements. In fact, some regress a bit.

That may be no surprise to their weary parents. But Arizona State University psychologists studying prosocial moral reasoning in children noted that it runs counter to most research, which shows a steady progression of altruistic thinking with age and maturity.

This longitudinal work on adolescents has provided a measure of how prosocial morals develop in adolescents. Meanwhile, it is being complemented by research elsewhere that compares mainstream teens with adolescents who have strong records of prosocial work, and by a study on high school juniors required to help feed the homeless.

Researchers historically have explored the development of moral reasoning by examining people's moral conflicts in fashioning rules, laws, and other formal obligations. But if those conditions are swept away or kept to a minimum, the adolescent is left to consider moral dilemmas in which one's own needs and wants directly conflict with another's.

By focusing on the latter types of dilemmas, researchers are beginning to understand teenagers' less-explored prosocial moral development.

Does Older Mean Nicer?

In general, positive moral reasoning advances with age. In the longitudinal work at Arizona State, adolescents approaching adulthood indeed used more self-reflective and internalized modes of moral reasoning.

From the *APA Monitor,* June 1996, p. 15.

To measure the reasoning process, participants were asked, for example, whether a hypothetical character named "Joe" should attend a birthday celebration or spend the time giving blood at a clinic. An internalized response might include the participants' thoughts on how Joe would feel about himself if he gave blood or not.

Researchers also gave the subjects a list of reasons why Joe should or shouldn't take the altruistic route, and asked the participants to rate the importance of each one. Among the different forms of reasoning being measured were: (a) stereotypic ("It depends on whether Joe thinks giving blood is the decent thing to do"); (b) hedonistic/reciprocal ("It depends how much fun the party would be") or ("It depends whether Joe will get paid to give blood"); (c) approval-oriented ("It depends whether Joe's parents and friends will think he did the right thing"); or (d) needs-oriented ("It depends whether the blood recipient really needs help or not").

They found that with age, reasoning—and hence, responses—become less stereotypic and less hedonistic, said Arizona State psychology professor Nancy Eisenberg, PhD, who is leading the longitudinal study.

"Reasoning becomes more sophisticated, abstract, and based on moral affect and on moral concerns," said Eisenberg.

But not always. Hedonistic reasoning, which steadily decreases in children as they approach early adolescence, shows a mild rise for some teens in mid-adolescence, Eisenberg and her colleagues found. After it flattens out in the midteen years, it rises again slightly in late adolescence, they said.

Approval-oriented reasoning and direct-reciprocity reasoning tailed off in early adolescence but then showed no decline into early adulthood, Eisenberg and her team reported in *Child Development*, August 1995.

The researchers used a variety of methods to collect their data over the years. For example, subjects were asked to solve moral dilemmas, then were retested years later on similar vignettes. In another test, subjects were paid $5 (four $1 bills and four quarters) for submitting to an interview, and then were told that the researcher belonged to a group raising money for a widely publicized child who needed a liver transplant. (The participants were not directly asked to donate to the cause.) Subjects were then left alone for one minute next to a donation box, giving them a chance to contribute money for the transplant if they so desired. Their donations were measured later.

Subjects were also asked how often they engaged in 23 behaviors, such as volunteering or giving money to charity. These and other re-search techniques, such as interviewing the subjects' mothers and at least one friend, gave the scientists a broad look at the adolescents' pro-social thinking.

Studies dating back to the 1960s show some apparent regression in moral judgement among teens. Eisenberg, who has worked with mostly white, middle-class adolescents during the 19-year study, sug-gested the late uptick in hedonistic and reciprocity-linked reasoning might stem from older adolescents' ability to cognitively evaluate the long-term costs of being altruistic. Younger adolescents are less likely to calculate the long-term ramifications, she said. And the older adoles-cents could just be more success-driven. The unusual trends were mainly seen in boys, she said.

In another odd finding, approval-related reasoning among adoles-cents age 17 to 19 didn't follow the pattern of decline that had prevailed to that point, Eisenberg said. That will require follow-up studies for clarification, she said. Also, the research needs to be conducted with people other than middle-class Caucasians, Eisenberg said. The study was authored by Eisenberg; Gustavo Carlo, PhD, an assistant professor of psychology at the University of Nebraska; Bridget Murphy; and Pa-tricia Van Court.

Sense of Self

Whereas the work of Eisenberg and her colleagues provides a long-term look at adolescents' moral development, other studies have taken in-triguing "snapshots" of such thinking in teens. One compares the views of highly motivated adolescents, who have records of community ser-vice, with their less-committed peers.

A strong sense of self seems to differentiate these highly committed adolescents from others who are less altruistic but still considered main-stream, said psychology professor Daniel Hart, EdD, of Rutgers Univer-sity. He is studying Latino and African-American adolescents in Cam-den, New Jersey, who have made unusually altruistic commitments to community groups. In Hart's research, 15 caring "exemplars" were matched with a control group of 15 other well-functioning adolescents from the same neighborhoods.

The subjects were interviewed about themselves and their moral judgements to gauge their understanding of self.

"The open-ended self-descriptions of the care exemplars contained more references to moral personality traits and to moral goals," Hart and Susan Fegley, a graduate psychology student at Temple University, wrote in *Child Development* in August 1995.

Also, the exemplars are less likely to emphasize distinctions between past and future versions of the self—an indication of greater stability and continuity—than the control group adolescents, Hart said. And the exemplars are more likely to identify their "ideal selves" with their actual selves, the researchers found. This suggested the exemplars are more oriented toward ideals and parental values than were the control group, who are more likely to orient toward peer values.

Also, more of the exemplars talked about personal beliefs and philosophies than did the controls, Hart and Fegley found.

Thus, no single factor, such as maturity, made one group more socially committed than the other, they concluded. The difference stemmed from a more complex array of views of the self.

Hart sought inner-city adolescents in Camden, an economically distressed city, and had little trouble finding exemplars for the study, who were recommended by church groups, school officials, and other members of the community.

"Adversity sharpens and reveals these commitments," he said. "They might not be quite as evident without the need."

Kitchen Patrol

James Youniss, PhD, took the opposite approach in his research on prosocial moral development. Rather than seek out committed adolescents who volunteer a lot, he studied inner-city adolescents who were *required* to take a high school class that involved some community service.[1]

Youniss, a professor of psychology at Catholic University, and Miranda Yates, PhD, a postdoctoral researcher at Brown University, tracked a group of predominantly African-American high school juniors through a social justice course in the Washington, DC area. The students were required to work at a soup kitchen for the needy at least four times during the semester. Afterward, they wrote essays on the experience.

Based on these writings and follow-up discussions with the students

---

[1]This study was published in the *Journal of Research on Adolescence, 6,* 1996, pp. 271–284.

in 1993 and 1994, Youniss and Yates found the adolescents raised moral issues with increasing sophistication as the semester unfolded. Their questions went beyond homelessness, for example, to wealth distribution in society.

"We are convinced they were thinking in moral terms and legal terms," Youniss said, noting that many of the moral discussions flowed into political ones.

By the end of their coursework, the students' behavior seemed changed. They had gone to the soup kitchen an average of seven times each, more than the required four, and some had volunteered even more often, Youniss said.

"These kids are in the process of developing their identity," he said. "Part of that identity is seeing yourself as a political or moral agent in society."

But contrary to looking at the identity as an inward search, he said, the experience seemed to push the adolescents to find their place in history, take ideological positions, identify with certain people and not others, and develop a context for finding a position in society.

6 Personality

Solitude Provides an Emotional Tune-Up

Hugh McIntosh

Conventional wisdom says that successful relationships are key to well-being and that solitude, consequently, may signal abnormality. But solitude seems to have a positive side, too.

For centuries poets, mystics, and philosophers have reported the soothing, creative effects of time alone. And in recent years, psychologists have begun to identify healthy people who partake of solitude for rejuvenation, contemplation, and other beneficial uses.

The need for solitude has both a state component and a trait component, according to psychologist Peter Suedfeld, PhD, of the University of British Columbia, who studies restricted environmental stimulation in lone voyages, polar stations, and other solitary situations.

Taking a Breather

Everyone experiences states where they need solitude more than at other times, he said. In addition, some people seem to have a trait for solitude, chronically wanting or needing it more than others do.

Research related to the state component of solitude suggests that most people have some need of time alone to satisfy any of several psychological needs, including rejuvenation. This need probably results from the cumulative effects of social stimulation over recent days or weeks, Suedfeld said. People with few demands and little social stimulation seem to need less solitude and, in fact, may avoid it. His research has found, however, that those with heavy demands on their attention,

From the *APA Monitor*, March 1996, pp. 1, 10.

social skills, or coping mechanisms—professors, business executives, mothers of small children—tend to need more time alone.

"It gives you a chance to restore your coping resources, to rest, relax," he said. It replenishes psychological energy and physical well-being, as measured by reduced stress hormones, improved immune functioning, and other physiological changes.

What one does during time alone—walking, meditation, systematic relaxation—seems less important for rejuvenation than simply achieving solitude. Convicts, he noted, sometimes hit a guard or break other rules in order to be put into solitary confinement, where they recoup from the hassle of prison life.

The amount of solitude people need for rejuvenation depends on how long it takes them to recover from the demands of their environment. An hour every few days may be enough to renew some people, although it may not be enough to achieve other benefits of solitude such as creative inspiration, Suedfeld said.

Time alone satisfies at least four other psychological needs, or functions, besides rejuvenation, says Darhl Pedersen of Brigham Young University. His research on privacy suggests that contemplation is the most important need fulfilled by solitude.

"It gives people a chance to contemplate who they are, what their relationships are to other people, and what their goals will be. It is a kind of settling and self-defining function."

Solitude also fosters creativity in self-actualizing people, he said, giving them a chance to speculate on new concepts without the censorship and evaluation that comes with putting forth ideas in public.

History shows, in fact, that people have long used solitude—voluntary or involuntary—for creativity. It appears, though, that creative solitude is not a time of particular happiness, according to psychologist Reed Larson, PhD, of the University of Illinois, whose research focuses on solitude in adolescents. He speculates that creative people are moderately lonely in solitude but feel activated. "They are probably into what they are doing." he said. "They might describe it at least sometimes as enthralling, sometimes as tormenting. But my guess is that they describe time with others as being their happy times."

Two other psychological needs that solitude meets are autonomy —"the chance to do your own thing, to act freely, and be who you are"—as well as "confiding," according to Pedersen. The latter, he said, was a somewhat surprising response from research subjects, who may use the term to describe a prayerful relationship with a deity. (Or, he said, subjects may have misunderstood the term "solitude" and assumed a confidante could be included.)

Pedersen's studies have found no gender differences in how often people seek solitude, he said. But they do indicate that women use solitude for contemplation and creativity more than men do. Men, on the other hand, have a stronger preference for isolation, a type of solitude where one geographically removes oneself from others by, for example, going up into the mountains or out for a long drive, rather than retreating to an office or bedroom.

The trait component of solitude suggests that some people have a preference for solitude that is much higher than the periodic need most people have for time alone. Psychologist Jerry Burger, PhD, of Santa Clara University speculates that only a small percentage of the population, perhaps no more than 10%, show this trait.

Contrary to social stereotypes, "these are folks who are well-adjusted," Burger said. "They're high in a sense of well-being or happiness, contentment with life." They are self-actualized, are good communicators, do well in social situations, and enjoy their friends. In addition, they like solitude, so they arrange time alone on a regular basis. "If they have to go several days without getting their 'fix' . . . they find that they don't feel as good."

This preference for solitude has a developmental aspect to it, appearing more frequently in people who have reached middle age, he said. It seems also to have a cyclical aspect. People need to develop a certain level of well-being in order to appreciate the benefits of solitude, and spending time alone helps to further develop well-being.

Children and Adolescents

Solitude appears to have salutary effects at other stages of development, particularly in adolescence. Adolescents report having higher concentration and lower self-consciousness during solitude, Larson said, suggesting a more productive mental state. After they've been alone, adolescents are in better moods than at other times. In addition, data indicate that adolescents who spend intermediate amounts of time alone—20% to 35% of waking hours—are better adjusted than those who spend more or less time alone.

Adolescents say they're lonely when they're by themselves, Larson said. But he distinguishes between the loneliness of solitude and loneliness relative to other people. "Feeling loneliness in relationship to friends is bad," he said. "But going off by yourself on a retreat or going to your room to be by yourself and feeling a little lonely, that's probably healthy."

In children, solitary play is often considered a sign of shyness. Children, however, play alone for many reasons, says psychologist Robert Coplan, PhD, of Carleton University. For most children, playing alone is the first step up the ladder toward playing with others. "The problem that we worry about is these children who never make it up to the next rung," he said.

In studies of preschoolers, Coplan and Kenneth Rubin, PhD, of the University of Maryland, have observed three different types of children who tend to play by themselves. One type is shy, wanting to interact with others but afraid or anxious about doing so. The second type is probably socially immature, a bit aggressive, active, and noisy, playing alone presumably because no one else wants to play with them. A third type, however, seems to enjoy playing alone in constructive ways, preferring toys, puzzles, and other objects to people.

"Kids who play alone in these kinds of constructive ways don't stick out in terms of indices of maladjustment," he said. "They're not more afraid. They're not more immature. Their parents don't rate them as more shy." They do, however, have longer attention spans than other children, and they do not do well with person-oriented tasks, such as playing show-and-tell.

"Right now, I don't think people can tell you for sure what happens to these kids when they grow up," he said. "But I would predict that most of them would become your every-day average kids."

Shy People Have Inaccurate Self-Concepts

Beth Azar

Jim dreams of going to a mixer and asking a woman to dance. Alex longs to be involved in a romance. Monica yearns for a promotion at work.

For shy people, these rather customary goals seem out of reach. Shy folks view themselves as socially inept and are painfully self-conscious when interacting with people. Simply telling them that their self-concept is wrong won't help either. They need help finding that out themselves.

Much of the work on the psychological treatment for shyness mirrors research on social phobia. Since 1982, Richard Heimberg, PhD, and his colleagues have been developing a cognitive-behavioral group therapy program to treat social phobia at the State University of New York, Albany's Center for Stress and Anxiety Disorders. Researchers and clinicians aiming to treat shyness have modeled programs after Heimberg's, modifying them as new research unfolds about the nature of shyness. The programs utilize role-playing to help acclimate shy people to social situations and analyze examples from their lives to give them a better perspective on their own abilities.

Dealing With Discrepancy

In cognitive-behavioral shyness treatment, patients learn to recognize the distortions in their self-concepts.

"We get [shy clients] to observe their own behavior," said Lynne Alden, PhD, professor of psychology at the University of British Colum-

From the *APA Monitor*, November 1995, p. 24.

bia with a clinical appointment at University Hospital. "They keep notes about their social interactions and how people respond to them."

They often see from the notes that they have inaccurate beliefs about themselves, she said. For example, a man came in for therapy after having to give a public speech. He said his presentation was terrible and that everyone could see his hands shaking violently. When Alden asked him for more details about the event, he conceded that a few people told him they enjoyed his speech, and that no one mentioned anything about his shaking hands.

"We try to pinpoint their dysfunctional beliefs and help them recognize them," said Alden.

Many of those beliefs center on a lack of social skills. However, most researchers agree shy people have the skills, but anxiety inhibits them. Psychologists need to help unlock them, Alden said.

To do that, treatment programs involving both group and individual therapy have clients act out scenes related to the particular fears that trigger their anxiety. In group therapy programs, clients work with each other as well as with outsiders. If someone wants to be able to ask someone for a date, they act it out; if they want to feel comfortable at a party, they practice mingling.

"Once they're in a role play, they realize they have more conversational and social skills than they think they have," said Lynne Henderson, PhD, director of Stanford University's Shyness Clinic and co-director of its Shyness Institute.

After clients become comfortable interacting during therapy, they're asked to try their new skills in real-life situations. Most become more comfortable in social situations and many meet their primary goals—accepting a promotion, asking someone on a date, or starting new friendships, said Alden.

Heimberg and his colleagues initially didn't anticipate the need to thoroughly debrief people after a role-play. Often people would be happy with their performance immediately after a role-play, but they would then sit and stew on it, picking it apart until they convinced themselves they'd failed, said Heimberg.

On the nights after the group met, Heimberg and his colleagues began getting late-night phone calls from patients who were depressed or even suicidal over their performance. Although his clients are more clinically disturbed than most shy clients, the tendency to put a negative spin on positive events is common.

"You'll ask a shy person what positive events happened over the past week and they'll say, 'Nothing'," Alden said. "Then you go moment by moment through their week and find some positive events."

That's when a therapist needs to step in and point out to them that, "Many people would say that having a woman give you her phone number is a positive event, but it seems to make you apprehensive. Why is that?" said Alden. "Therapists have a tendency to look for events the patient didn't handle well and to accept the patient's negative view of themselves. But they would be surprised at the number of opportunities for success, such as social invitations and situations the patient handled well. This is what the patient needs to recognize."

In some basic research, Heimberg and Henderson found that shy people tend to blame themselves for failure and credit others for success. This compounds an already negative self-image, said Henderson.

After each interaction they feel shame because they failed and blame themselves for being inadequate. Shame kills their motivation to try again, she said. She's seen people get better in social interactions, deny their success, and return to old behaviors.

The Sensitive Clinician

A cool, distant, or overly directive therapist is likely to lose shy patients, said Alden. She's found that therapists need to be exceptionally warm and supportive, drawing patients out to set their own goals and direct their own progress.

Shy people have learned to erase themselves: They avoid eye contact, speak softly or less than others, and rarely take a strong position on a topic. They tend to wait for the therapist to figure out their problems and often decline to correct a wrong assumption, said Alden. Therapists must overcome the tendency to take charge and do all the talking and instead provide an atmosphere where patients feel comfortable speaking for themselves.

"We use the events of the person's life to help them see their beliefs aren't accurate," said Alden.

She recalls a client who was a research technician who never talked to anyone at work and always refused invitations to have coffee with his co-workers. She assigned him to talk to the woman who sat next to him at the lab. He feared the woman would snub him, but when he mustered the courage to speak to her, she was at first surprised and then responsive and friendly. He then went out for coffee with co-workers, and was able to actively participate in the conversation. This helped him recognize that his fears were unwarranted.

Many people who undergo this treatment become better able to interact with people at home, in public, and at work, researchers say. However, few will probably become extroverts and many will occasionally suffer from some type of social anxiety, they add.

Henderson promotes a wellness model of social interaction. Not everyone can be a star athlete but they can find a comfortable fitness program. Likewise, not everyone can be a star socialite, but they can become comfortable with daily interactions.

Timidity Can Develop in the First Days of Life

Beth Azar

Does your mother love to remind you how much you cried as a baby, scared of everything, forever cranky? Or were you always smiling, impervious to the constant sensory stimulation coming at you? As you aged, did you hide behind your mother's skirt or did you make friends with everyone you met?

Your behaviors back then may have predicted who you are now—shy and inhibited, gregarious and extroverted, or somewhere in between, according to a series of studies by psychologists. Shyness takes many routes and for some the journey may begin with an inborn temperament that makes them emotionally vulnerable, say researchers such as Jerome Kagan, PhD, of Harvard University and Nathan Fox, PhD, of the University of Maryland.

Physiological Clues

Some babies are more reactive to sights, sounds, and smells. They fidget and cry more than other babies, especially when thrust into new and unfamiliar environments. Researchers can recognize distinct temperaments among babies as young as 4 months.

The extremes—the top and bottom 20% of babies in the United States—are what psychologists call high and low reactive. High-reactive babies respond to a colored toy or recording of a woman's voice with lots of motor activity. The low reactors, of the same age, family background, and health status, barely react at all. Fox has found that among

From the *APA Monitor*, November 1995, p. 23.

the high-reactive babies, some are fearful, responding with distress and crying, and others appear happy and alert.

Both researchers are following several large groups of children to see how their early temperaments affect their personalities and to see what factors seem to affect this progression.

Kagan finds that, as they grow, the high-reactive children are more likely to hide behind their mothers' skirts in a room full of adults, while low-reactive children are likely to be sociable and bold. Fox expanded those findings to show that it is the high-reactive, distressed babies who become shy. The high-reactive alert babies tend to become highly sociable, outgoing, and sometimes aggressive. In this article "high-reactive" refers to high-reactive *fearful* children.

To account for the contrasting developmental paths in otherwise similar children, researchers have turned to physiology. They theorize that babies who react with activity and distress to novel events are different physiologically from children who react with complacence.

In fact, 4-month-old high-reactive babies have significantly faster heart rates than low-reactive babies when resting and when they encounter something new, Fox and Kagan have found. Kagan has measured heart rates *in utero* and finds that babies with fast prenatal heart rates tend to develop into high-reactive, fearful children. High-reactive children also startle more easily, said Fox.

One cause of fear-like responses in these children may lie in humans' evolutionary history, said Kagan. Based on studies of animals, researchers believe the brain's right hemisphere participates more in fear states. Temperament researchers have found much more EEG activity (electric signaling) in the right hemispheres of high-reactive kids than low-reactive kids. Also, high-reactive children had cooler brow temperatures and cooler right-finger temperatures than low-reactive kids. Both of these findings indicate greater right-sided brain activity.

"There may be an underlying functional reason that all these measures are responding the way they are," said Fox.

The answer lies in the brain's emotion and information processing centers. Fox and Kagan posit that differences in brain chemistry may affect how easily excited these areas become when a child encounters new things, like a loud noise or new toy. These processing centers are linked to the sympathetic nervous system, which controls such involuntary bodily functions as heartbeat, breathing, and blood flow. These circuits activate more easily in high-reactive kids and when activated, the kids feel uncertainty and distress, fear and anxiety, said Fox. In infancy the distress manifests as crying and fidgeting. Toddlers, who are better able to regulate their reactions, withdraw socially, and try to avoid new situations.

Both Kagan and Fox have found that most high-reactive 4-month-old babies continue to show physiological differences, such as faster heart rate and right-sided brain activity, as they age and are likely to be fearful, shy, and subdued at ages 2, 3, and 4. Babies who remain quiet or motionless during novel events are likely to become sociable and bold.

But not all fearful infants grow up shy or withdrawn, and not all calm infants remain complacent as they mature, said Kagan. "Personality grows out of temperament and experience," he said.

Kagan has found that high-reactive babies don't have to become shy as they age. They can be reasonably social but are less likely to become extremely bold and exuberant. Furthermore, low-reactive babies can look less than exuberant, but rarely look extremely shy and fearful.

Overcoming Timidity

Fox has preliminary evidence that suggests which home environments help children overcome their temperamental tendency toward shyness. He started with his first group of fearful children, now age 7. He showed them a video of fearful inhibited toddlers and asked them if they thought they were like the child in the video. Most said no. He then showed them videos of themselves as toddlers and asked them to explain the discrepancy between themselves as babies and their current self-concept.

Some continued to deny they were fearful. Others admitted they were still fearful. In the most telling group, subjects admitted that they were once fearful, but articulately explained their transformation, Fox said. Most said the change occurred because of the supportive environment their parents provided, said Fox. For example, they reported, "My parents helped by not making me do things I was scared of," or "My parents introduced me to new things slowly."

This anecdotal evidence gave Fox the kernel of a hypothesis: Parents can help their kids overcome a physiological predisposition to be shy and inhibited by providing a supportive home environment that recognizes fearfulness and shyness and that helps the child go at his or her own pace.

He's following this up with a scientific study that looks specifically at how home environment and mother–child interactions affect personality development. He also continues to analyze his physiological data on the 7-year-olds to see if it matches their professed changes in temperament.

These are the extreme cases of temperament, and represent only a fraction of children who grow up to become shy adults, admit Fox and Kagan.

However, the research reveals the role physiology plays in behavior. The baby may not simply be cranky, but also overloaded by novelty. And the toddler may not simply be finicky, but may be trying to deal with uncertainty.

Social

Evolution Shapes Our Ability to Spot Cheaters

Beth Azar

A group of evolutionary psychologists believe that our ability to spot when someone's cheating—either breaking a deal or violating a rule—was shaped by the same evolutionary process that designed adaptive physical features, such as an opposable thumb and erect posture.

And these researchers believe that other reasoning skills, such as the abilities to recognize danger and threats, are also evolved adaptations. They argue that natural selection precipitated at least three distinct inference pathways, each specialized for reasoning about one of these domains.

Not everyone argues that our reasoning abilities derive from such Darwinian forces. For instance, another group of researchers believes that we simply learn these skills as children and that several broad reasoning mechanisms handle a large range of problems, including one that encompasses danger, threats, and cheating alike.

But evolutionary backers have powerful evidence on their side: Standardized reasoning tasks show that people around the world reason more accurately when facing deceit and danger than when facing a problem that would have been unimportant to our prehistoric ancestors.

A Test of Reason

At this point both perspectives are just theories. And both camps rely on similar lines of evidence for support. Indeed, their studies are largely

From the *APA Monitor*, August 1996, p. 31.

based on how people solve variations of the same test—the Wason selection task.

The test, developed 30 years ago by Peter Wason, PhD, measures logical reasoning skills. In the standard version, people learn a basic rule applied to a set of cards with letters on one side and numbers on the other. A typical rule reads: *If a card has an "A" on one side, then it has a "1" on the other side.* Participants then see the tops of four cards, which might show an "A," a "1," a "B," and a "3." They must choose the best and fewest cards they need to turn over to tell if the rule is being followed.

The correct answer is "A" and "3." That's because the rule is a conditional—"If *p* then *q*"—and the logical way to prove any conditional is the same: Choose *p* and not *q*, or, for the example, *A* and *not 1*. However, fewer than 10% of people typically answer correctly with this abstract version of the task. Instead, they often select illogical patterns, such as "A" and "1."

Since Wason first realized people have problems with this task, many researchers have used variations to study cognitive reasoning.

Cheater Detectors

University of California, Santa Barbara psychologist Leda Cosmides, PhD, and her anthropologist husband John Tooby, PhD, considered the types of problems our evolutionary ancestors would have needed to successfully overcome to survive. For one, they would have needed to understand the rules of social exchange and how to detect someone breaking those rules, said Cosmides.

She and Tooby define social exchange as a transaction in which one person offers another a benefit that is contingent on something else. For example, *I'll mow your lawn, if you give me $5.*

To study whether we have mechanisms designed to spot cheaters, they devised a series of experiments. In one, they told people a long story about a Polynesian tribe and a rule the tribe established: *If a man eats cassava root, then he must have a tattoo on his face.* As with the standard Wason task, people are faced with four cards. One side of each card describes the food a man is eating, and the other side says whether he has a tattooed face or not. Participants can only see one side of each card. What they see is: *eats cassava root, tattoo, no tattoo,* and *eats molo nuts.*

They must then choose which is the best of the four cards to flip to prove that no one is violating the rule. About 75% of people correctly turned over the cards that read *eats cassava root* and *no tattoo*.

From this and similar studies, Cosmides and Tooby conclude that the human brain has mechanisms that make us good at detecting cheaters. However, these studies do not, by themselves, prove that we have a specific mechanism designed just for this purpose.

One way to establish this is to show that people are good at detecting violations of social contracts when these are caused by cheating—illicitly taking benefits—but not when they are caused by innocent mistakes.

With that in mind, they used the same card test to design an experiment that gave two groups of people the same rule, but different expectations. They told participants that the county school board was sorting high school entrance forms from two towns: Grover City and Hanover. Grover City has high taxes and good schools, while Hanover has low taxes and poor schools. The rule for sorting forms was, *If a student is to be assigned to Grover High School, then that student must live in Grover City.*

One group heard that mothers of high school children sorted student forms and might have cheated, assigning some students to the wrong school. The second group learned that an absent-minded elderly woman from the board of education separated the forms and might have made some mistakes. In both cases participants had to determine if any of four students had been placed in the wrong school.

The problem was essentially the same for both groups. However, 68% of participants who thought the mother sorted the forms, knew how to detect if she followed the rule. But only 27% of the other group made the same determination about the old woman, said Cosmides.

The old woman had nothing to gain from her mistakes so people's "cheater detector" mechanism wasn't triggered, Cosmides explained.

These results seem to contradict reasoning theories, which assert that a few broad mechanisms handle a large range of reasoning problems. Keith Holyoak, PhD, and Patricia Cheng, PhD, of the University of California, Los Angeles, believe that people do well at deductive reasoning tasks that conform to common societal rules, in the form of "permissions," "obligations," and "causations."

For example, from infancy we are exposed to obligation rules such as, *if you want dessert, you must first eat your dinner* and permission rules such as, *if you stay quiet, you can have some candy.* These broad types of rules become so ingrained that when a situation fits into one of the patterns, it triggers an automatic reasoning response.

Holyoak and Cheng believe the "social exchange" problems Cosmides and Tooby examine are simply a subset of permissions, obligations, and causations. For example, they would call the Grover City High rule an obligation. As for the reason people's responses changed based on who they thought was sorting the forms, Cheng and Holyoak suggest that Cosmide's experimental materials failed to make it clear to participants in the elderly woman paradigm that the rule was a conditional permission. Without that, they contend, the correct response isn't triggered.

What About Perspective?

Gerd Gigerenzer, PhD, of the Max Planck Institute for Psychological Research in Munich and others have also found that perspective plays a big part in people's reasoning in these situations. Gigerenzer gave people the rule: *If an employee works for 10 years, he or she must receive a full pension.* He then told some people to imagine that they were the company owner and others to imagine that they were employees. The test cards represented four employees and read, *worked 10 years, no pension, worked less than 10 years* and *receives pension.*

When asked to turn over the cards that proved the rule had not been violated, "owners" chose *worked less than 10 years* and *receives a pension.* In contrast, "employees" chose *worked 10 years* and *no pension.* In other words, owners define cheating as an employee who receives a pension without earning it. But employees define cheating as an employer who denies a pension to someone who deserves it.

Cosmides and Holyoak each believe that such studies confirm their theories. For Cosmides, it makes sense that we would have evolved the ability to look for cheating that best matches our goals. And Holyoak's and Cheng's theory predicts that perspective will affect the interpretation of the rule and therefore change the form of the reasoning response.

Other researchers, including British researchers Ken Manktelow, PhD, and David Over, PhD, have found that people are also good at interpreting rules related to taking precautions. Cosmides and Tooby believe they have data showing that people have separate mechanisms for interpreting such precaution rules as well as for interpreting threats.

One of their graduate students has given Wason tests to a group of Shiwiar, a remote aboriginal tribe in Ecuador. Shiwiar show the same "cheater detection" response even though their social world is drastically different from our own, said Cosmides. If general purpose learning were responsible, it would be strange to find the same reasoning mechanisms developing in such different cultures, she argues.

TV Displays Violence Without the Mess

Nathan Seppa

In the movie, *The Purple Rose of Cairo*, the hero is a well-coiffed actor who grows tired of being shown on the same movie screen night after night. So the celluloid star steps off the screen into real life and runs off with a woman he meets in the movie-house audience. Events take a turn for the worse when he endures a nasty beating by her jealous husband.

But moments later the hero character hops to his feet, unscathed. "I'm fine," he tells his astonished friend. "I don't get hurt or bleed. My hair doesn't muss. It's one of the advantages of being imaginary."

People studying television violence know what he's talking about, and for them it's no laughing matter. Psychologists have said for years that the consequences of violence on the screen are often glossed over. Now, a new study bears this out in detail. Research conducted by psychologists at the University of California (UC)-Santa Barbara and three other universities over the past two years has found that 58% of violent acts on TV depict no painful consequences of the violence (see Figure 2), while 47% don't show any harm to victims at all. Such programming risks desensitizing viewers to the realities of violence, other research has shown.

The study also found that violence on TV often goes unpunished and results in no long-term consequences for the characters depicted, particularly in children's programming. And few TV programs have an antiviolence theme, the study said.

The researchers recommended that the TV industry cut back on violence, move it to later time slots, include consequences of depicted violence, boost nonviolent heroes, use more codes and advisories, and

From the *APA Monitor*, April 1996, p. 8.

Figure 2

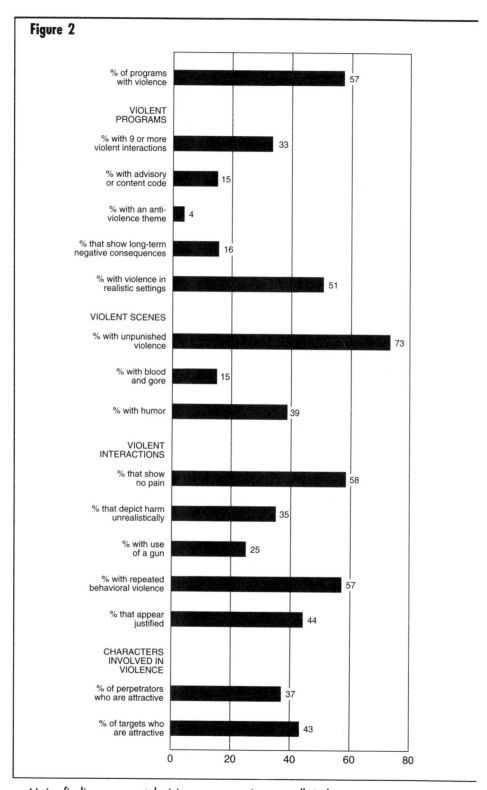

Major findings across television programming overall: Industry averages.

air more antiviolence public service announcements. The study, conceived by Sen. Paul Simon (D-Ill.) after congressional hearings and his threat of government regulation in the early 1990s, was funded by the National Cable Television Association. It concentrated on the context of TV violence and analyzed the nature and extent of violent episodes. Context includes whether a victim suffers visibly, whether the violence was committed by a hero or villain, whether it was shown close up or from a distance, and whether a weapon was present.

The study was based on three well-understood effects of viewing TV violence: learning to behave more aggressively or harmfully toward others, becoming more fearful of the world, and getting desensitized to violence.

The research included a review of past TV-violence studies, preparation of an extensive code book to define violence, a random sampling of 23 channels between 6 AM and 11 PM by researchers, an analysis of program content, a study of ratings and advisories, an assessment of antiviolence messages, and a compilation of recommendations.

Romeo and Juliet

The researchers went beyond network shows and prime-time slots to track random samples of all TV programming, including movies on broadcast, basic cable, and premium cable channels. The team crafted a specific definition of violence: physically violent acts; harmful consequences that may have happened off-camera, such as a dead person who clearly died by intended violence; and credible threats of violence, such as a mugger brandishing a gun.

Of keen interest was the message being sent by a program. For example, if a police officer shoots someone and winds up in counseling by the end of the program, that sends a different message from a show that only shows the shooting, said Edward Donnerstein, PhD, a psychologist at UC-Santa Barbara and one of the study's investigators.

"Keep in mind Romeo and Juliet came out antiviolent in our analysis" because the basic message is the tragic consequences of violence, he said. Similarly, the movie *Schindler's List* contains violent scenes, but its point—to expose the horrors of a Nazi concentration camp—is clearly antiviolent. By factoring in context, Donnerstein said, the researchers went beyond body counts to measure more precisely which programming sent a violent message or glorified violence.

The study also found:

- Handguns are involved in one fourth of all violent interactions on TV.
- Perpetrators go unpunished in 73% of violent scenes.
- Only 16% of all programs show long-term repercussions of violence.
- Public broadcasting offers the least violence (in 18% of its programming), broadcast networks show more (in 44%), and premium cable channels have the most (in 85%).
- Movies are the most likely medium to depict violence in realistic terms, such as with blood. Children's programs are the least likely to deal realistically with violence, with only 5% showing any long-term consequences of violence and two thirds depicting violence as humorous.

The researchers also found that most violent movies on premium channels have "viewer discretion" warnings, but that few other TV programs carry them. While such ratings are useful for parents, they can have unintended effects on children. For example, adolescent boys rejected movies rated G and showed much more interest in those rated PG-13 or R, the study found. Also, the "parental discretion" warning tended to attract boys ages 10 to 14, rather than being a deterrent. But girls, particularly those ages 5 to 9, showed less interest in a show if it got such a warning.

Industry Backing

Psychologist Ron Slaby, PhD, of Harvard University, said the study could provide guidance for the TV industry as it installs "V-chips" into most new sets, as required in the telecommunications bill signed by President Clinton in February 1996. V-chips enable viewers to block certain programs. Establishing a system of ratings to be used in conjunction with the chip will require good definitions of violence, Slaby said, which this study could provide.

The cable-TV industry deserves credit for backing the research, said Leonard Eron, PhD, a professor of psychology at the University of Michigan.

"Now that they've financed the study themselves, they can't accuse the researchers of being biased," said Eron.

"We welcome this landmark study as an important step in addressing our ongoing concerns as an industry about violence on television," said National Cable Television Association President Decker Anstrom.

Senior researchers on the study from UC-Santa Barbara were Donnerstein, Dale Kunkel, PhD, Dan Linz, PhD, James Potter, PhD, and Barbara Wilson, PhD; from the University of Texas, Wayne Danielson, PhD, Dominic Lasorsa, PhD, Ellen Wartella, PhD, and Charles Whitney; from the University of Wisconsin, Joanne Cantor, PhD; and from the University of North Carolina, Frank Biocca, PhD, and Jane Brown, PhD.

Police Tactics May Border on Coercion

Beth Azar

What would make an innocent person confess to a rape or murder? Psychologists assert that the legal techniques some police use to interrogate crime suspects can prompt such false confessions and impede justice.

Subtle techniques can induce some people to not only confess to doing something they didn't do, but to believe they did it, according to psychologist Saul Kassin, PhD, of Williams College. Kassin cites data from the first experimental study on false confessions: He accused intelligent, self-assured college students of committing a prohibited act. Even though none of them had done it, after subtle coercion many confessed that they had and some even believed that they had.

The Anatomy of a Confession

A confession is the single strongest piece of evidence a prosecutor can present, said Kassin. Even when there is conflicting evidence, juries and judges are more likely to convict a suspect when he or she has confessed. The only defense to a confession is to say it was coerced—that's where psychology steps in.

The law disallows any confession prompted by threats, physical violence, or promises of lenience. But the law does not address forms of less blatant coercion, and police may use more subtle techniques. For example, they may increase tension during interrogations by putting suspects in a sound-proof, starkly furnished room and sitting a little closer than comfortable. They use scare tactics, such as exaggerating or lying about evidence or exaggerating the severity of the crime. Or, they feign sympathy for the suspect, underplaying the seriousness of the

From the *APA Monitor*, October 1995, p. 27.

crime and taking the blame off the suspect by blaming the victim for provoking the crime—"she was asking to be raped, wearing that tight skirt."

Kassin and other social psychologists say these techniques can be just as influential as blatant coercion. Research shows that people imply threats or leniency from the legal techniques just as much as from the more explicit but illegal techniques.

"In essence, these ploys, which are common in practice, are used to circumvent the laws that prohibit the use of coerced confessions," said Kassin.

Although there have been no systematic studies to determine how often innocent people falsely confess to crimes, there are many documented instances, said Kassin. Based on real-life examples, Kassin and psychologist Larry Wrightsman, PhD, identified three distinct types of false confessions:

- *voluntary,* involving no external pressure;
- *coerced–compliant,* involving someone who knows he or she is innocent, but confesses to receive a promised reward or avoid an aversive situation; and
- *coerced–internalized,* involving someone who comes to believe that he or she is truly guilty.

It's the second two that Kassin is particularly interested in and that law enforcement and court officials have the hardest time believing. They doubt that authorities can convince innocent people that they committed a crime.

Proof Positive

In his study, Kassin set out to determine whether memories for one's own actions can be altered. He and his student, Catherine L. Kiechel, designed an experiment to test the hypothesis that presenting false evidence can lead vulnerable people to confess to an act they didn't commit.

They invited 75 college students to participate in a simple reaction-time experiment. Each subject had to type a series of letters read aloud by another student (a clandestine confederate working with the experimenter) as fast as possible into a computer. Before beginning, the experimenter warned the typist not to press the ALT key on the keyboard because the computer would crash and data would be lost.

One minute into each experiment, the computer crashed and the experimenter jumped up accusing the typist of pressing the forbidden key. None actually did, as evidenced by video tapes, and every subject adamantly denied the accusation.

Kassin manipulated subjects' vulnerability to doubting their own innocence by varying the pace the confederate read the letters: either a slow 43 letters per minute or a frenzied 67 letters per minute. Also, in half the cases the confederate presented false evidence by claiming to have seen the subject hit the ALT key.

To see if subjects could be coerced into confessing, the experimenter handwrote a standard confession note—"I hit the ALT key and caused the program to crash. Data were lost." Then he prodded subjects to sign it, asking up to two times. The consequence would be an angry phone call from Kassin.

Close to two thirds of all students signed the note with percentages increasing depending on their vulnerability. The most vulnerable students were typing fast and had a "witness" to their mistake; 100% of them signed the note. Eighty-nine percent of the slow-paced students with a witness signed. Results for students without witnesses were 65% for the fast-paced and 35% for the slow-paced students.

Compliance was probably so high because, for ethical reasons, the researchers used a situation without serious consequence that merely accused people of negligence as opposed to criminal intent, said Kassin. More important findings came from tests of whether the researchers could get students to believe they committed the "crime."

To measure feelings of guilt, the researchers continued the farce. As the subject and experimenter left the lab, they ran into a subject waiting to enter—really another confederate—who had overheard the commotion. The experimenter left the subject alone with the confederate who asked what happened. A hidden recorder taped the response.

Overall, 28% of the students believed they were guilty, saying things like, "I hit the wrong button and ruined the program." Broken down by group, 65% of the fast-paced witnessed subjects thought they were guilty, as did 44% of the slow-paced witnessed subjects, and 12% of the fast-paced unwitnessed subjects.

To see if any of the subjects were convinced enough of their guilt to "recall" when they hit the ALT key, the researchers brought them back into the lab and asked them to reconstruct their actions. A full 35% of the fast-paced witnessed subjects confabulated details to support their guilt, saying things like "I hit it with the side of my hand right after you called out the 'A'."

"This study provides strong support for a provocative hypothesis, that people can be induced to internalize guilt for an outcome they did not produce—and that the risk is increased by the use of false evidence, a trick used often by the police and accepted by many courts," said Kassin.

Gender and Diversity

Fathers Strongly Influenced by Culture

Tori DeAngelis

When scores of men descended on Washington, DC, in October 1995 for the "Million Man March," one message they heard from Nation of Islam leader Louis Farrakhan concerned their roles as fathers. Men should be responsible for their children and families, he exhorted, and resume their rightful places as heads of the household.

But what are their rightful places? Psychological research conducted in the past two decades paints a varied answer to that question. While some politicians trumpet the notion that fathers are necessary to families for their unique masculine qualities, research shows that parenting styles are often infuenced by culture. And while fathers are indeed important to families, it's not necessarily because they have qualities different from those that make some women good parents.

"Most of what parents provide that has important consequences for children does not come in gender-differentiated categories," says Joseph Pleck, PhD, a social and developmental psychologist at the University of Illinois at Urbana-Champaign, who has conducted numerous studies on parenting. "But there are common elements that make up good parenting, no matter what gender you are, such as responsiveness, sensitivity, empathy, and good judgment."

Men's Emphatic Reactions

But men and women learn different roles that can squelch men's expression of empathy and connection early on, psychologists say. While all children start out as emotionally responsive, by age 6 boys have learned to actively suppress their emotions, according to research by University of Connecticut psychologist Buck Park, PhD.

From the *APA Monitor*, April 1996, pp. 1, 39.

A study conducted in the 1980s bears that finding out in adults: Psychologist Fran Grossman, PhD, found that men and women have the same empathic reactions to hearing their newborn babies cry, although their responses appear totally different. The women rush in to quell the infants' distress, while the men sit by impassively.

But when men's stress levels were tested by measuring their galvanic skin responses, they "were off the charts physiologically," showing much higher rates of agitation than the women, said psychologist William Pollack, PhD, director of the Center for Men at McClean Hospital, Harvard Medical School's teaching hospital.

A related study by Lamb found that men and women are both equally clumsy as parents when a baby is born. A year later, though, mothers appear much more competent than fathers. But that's entirely because they've spent more time with the babies than the men, he said.

The way tests are constructed can also make men and women appear to have different parenting styles, Pollack said. A study he ran, for instance, found that men tested lower on empathy than women. But on closer inspection, the measures for empathy turned out to be female-based, examining such factors as how often parents talked to or held their babies. Since men characteristically show caring by taking action to fix distressing situations, their version of empathy wasn't tapped by the scale. Pollack is now conducting long-term field research on fathers to examine directly how they show caring and involvement with their children.

Testing the Theory

An intriguing way to test the theory of innate gender-based parenting modes is to examine child-rearing practices in different cultures, and among nonhuman primates. Male monkeys and apes show a tremendous variability in fathering behavior, said Louise Silverstein, PhD, of Yeshiva University. In a species of marmosets, for instance, the father is involved in everything but breast-feeding, she said. Because marmosets always have twins and the babies are proportionately large compared to the parents, delivering babies can leave the mother exhausted.

"The father has to be the full-time nurturer—he really is responsible for the infant care," she said.

But chimpanzees are minimally involved in fathering their young, she said.

Research also shows that male monkeys can learn to parent, Silverstein said. She cites a study conducted by psychologist Steven Suomi, PhD, of the University of Wisconsin, which found that when male and female adolescent rhesus monkeys were put in a cage with a baby monkey, the female acted as the infant's mother, feeding and caring for it. But when the female was removed from the cage, the male took over the nurturing behavior.

Even the issue of "rough-and-tumble play"—playful roughhousing with youngsters often cited as more characteristic of men—is an open question. Traditionalists in the men's movement argue that such play is a demonstration of fathers' more physical style.

But when social scientists began to explore the issue cross-culturally in humans, they found that fathers in Sweden and in hunter-gatherer societies rarely engage in rough play, said Silverstein. Anthropologist Barry Hewlett, PhD, looked for the style among African aborigines, and found that *aunts* were the ones to engage in such play with young children.

"The purpose of rough-and-tumble play seems to be to reignite an adult's attachment to a child—a notion partly borne out of anecdotes about working moms who engage in such play with their children when they return from business trips," she said.

Equal but Different?

The qualities of affiliation and autonomy are often cited as examples of how men and women parent differently. Women are supposed to help the family connect, while fathers encourage their children's autonomy. As discussed in his book *In a Time of Fallen Heroes: The Re-Creation of Masculinity* (Guilford Press, 1993), coauthored with R. William Belcher, PhD, MD, Pollack's research challenges that more traditional view.

Both genders had qualities of autonomy and affiliation, he found. But men and women differed in how they *perceived* the two qualities: Men said they affiliated with their children by playing with or teaching them, while women did so through hugging and holding.

"We need to recognize that there is a *his* autonomy and a *her* autonomy, a *his* intimacy and a *her* intimacy, to read between the lines when each seems to be speaking the same language," Pollack and Belcher write.

Not all psychologists think men and women are alike as parents.

Psychologist Wade Horn, PhD, believes that men and women have different biologies, different instincts.

"Using androgyny as a goal is very disturbing for the family and the well-being of children," says Horn, a former commissioner for Children, Youth, and Family Services under President Bush and director of the National Fatherhood Initiative, a Lancaster, Pennsylvania-based organization set up to foster a responsible fatherhood agenda. "It's a very uninspiring message for men" because it does not emphasize their special contributions, he said.

While the notion of a unique fathering style is questionable empirically, it may help some men participate more fully in fatherhood, Pleck said. And the more fathers are involved positively and nonabusively with their children, he said, the better off their kids are—no matter what their style.

Gender Gap in Math Scores Is Closing

Bridget Murray

Boys have historically outscored girls on the mathematical sections of national achievement tests, fueling the age-old debate about whether socialization or biology accounts for the performance difference. But, except at the highest levels of analytical thinking, the gender gap in mathematical performance is narrowing, according to psychologists and testing experts.

Thirteen-year-old girls have practically caught up to boys in their adeptness at intermediate math involving moderately complex procedures and reasoning, such as geometry and simple algebra, according to a recent report from the Educational Testing Service, the nation's largest private educational measurement institution.

In 1992, 59% of girls versus 60% of boys had reached that intermediate level, compared with 48% of girls versus 55% of boys in 1973.

During the same period, nine-year-old boys and girls exhibited equal ability to solve basic problems. But at age 17, boys remained ahead of girls in their ability to solve complex algebraic and precalculus problems. Roughly 10% of boys reach the most complex level compared with 5% of girls.

The findings derive from testing by the government-based National Assessment of Educational Progress, also known as America's Report Card, which has tracked trends in students' academic achievement for the National Center for Education Statistics since 1973.

"Girls are doing better at math [than before], but boys are still aiming higher because more of them want to make a career of it," said Ina Mullis, PhD, an education professor at Boston College and a coauthor of the ETS report. "As a result, we're still seeing a career gap for men and women."

From the *APA Monitor*, November 1995, p. 43.

A 1990 meta-analysis of gender differences in math performance backs the Report Card findings. Janet Hyde, PhD, and Elizabeth Fennema, PhD, of the University of Wisconsin-Madison, examined 100 studies covering national achievement testing of 3 million people and found that males barely outperformed females at math.

A similar meta-analysis released this year by Larry Hedges, PhD, and his student Amy Nowell, of the University of Chicago, also showed boys with an unremarkable mathematical edge on girls. Moreover, Hyde's analysis suggests that at all ages and levels, girls and boys showed similar understanding of math concepts, and that girls actually surpass boys in computation before high school. But in high school, boys show more skill at solving complex problems.

"Some people think boys are better at math at all levels," Hyde said. "We found no evidence of that. It's not until high school that boys pull ahead."

In debating reasons for the disparity at the top, psychologists and educators have offered myriad nature-versus-nurture explanations.

Is It Variability?

Some psychologists propose a score-variability hypothesis. They contend that a greater disparity in math ability among boys compared with girls explains boys' higher scores on complex problems. They note that more boys score higher as well as lower in math than girls and that there are more male geniuses *and* more males with developmental disabilities in the general population.

More boys than girls consistently show up in the Iowa State precocious youth study, which selects 13- to 15-year-olds with high math SAT scores.

Also, Hedges and Nowell found more male variance in their meta-analysis of six large data sets collected from tests of adolescents' cognitive abilities. Males generally scored higher than females in all areas except reading comprehension, perceptual speed, and associative memory. More males scored lower than females, as well. For instance, on the analytic reasoning section of one national test, almost twice as many males as females were in the bottom 10%.

. . . or Biology?

Psychologist Doreen Kimura, PhD, at the University of Western Ontario, attributes much of the difference to biology. Men are, on average, better at math reasoning, she argues.

Her research suggests a hormonal contribution to math ability, she says. Her 1991 study on 88 college students, for example, suggests that women with high testosterone levels and men with low testosterone levels have higher spatial and mathematical ability than low testosterone women and high testosterone men. She has also found differences in the way men and women think. In a 1993 study of nearly 100 under-graduates' map-route learning, for example, men took more direct routes and made fewer errors, while women relied more on landmarks and made more errors.

Brainwaves, rather than hormones, could cause men to dominate the higher end of the math spectrum, some speculate. Based on her findings in an ongoing study of mathematically precocious youth, Iowa State University psychologist Camilla Benbow, PhD, suggests that highly intelligent boys and girls differ in the way their brains approach spatial activities.

In the study of 40 youth, researchers asked boys and girls to perform a specified spatial task—judging such facial expressions as happy, sad, angry, or perplexed. The researchers found that boys had higher activity in the right hemisphere of their brains than girls.

But Hyde discounts both biological and variability hypotheses, faulting the biological explanations for being unreplicable, and the variability hypothesis for being purely descriptive and failing to describe the causes of the variability. In keeping with Hyde's meta-analysis, Benbow notes an important distinction between math performance and reasoning: Girls usually *perform* better than boys, often earning higher grades, while boys *reason* better than girls at the highest mathematical levels. Nature and nurture work together to produce this pattern.

"We need to work on nurturing girls' reasoning skills," said Benbow, noting that girls in high school select fewer math courses than boys.

. . . or Course Choice?

The real issue is gender differences in course choice, not math ability, said Hyde. Girls opt out of tougher high-school math courses, which explains their lower scores on standardized tests, she believes.

While Benbow links girls' math avoidance with a dislike for math, Hyde and other psychologists view gender conditioning by parents, teachers, and society as the real culprit.

"Girls hear a message that math won't be as valuable for their futures as boys' and they have lower expectations for success than boys," said Hyde.

Psychologist Jacquelynne Eccles, PhD, has seen strong parental influences as she's tracked students from more than 2,000 families in southeastern Michigan schools. In a 1990 finding, she noted that parents' gender stereotyping influenced kids' own self-perceptions. This in turn influenced students' course selection. By high school, more boys participated in sports, and made honors in math and physics than girls. Some of this sex-typing was even evident by the second and third grades.

Girls are also more likely than boys to view themselves as unskilled at math and, as a result, avoid it, said Eccles, who is based at the University of Michigan Institute for Social Research. Because girls place a low value on math, they avoid optional math courses in high school, she asserted.

Gender stereotypes lead more girls to view English and other verbal courses as more important than math and science courses for their future careers. Schools can help change those preconceived notions, pointing out that even careers in the social sciences require solid math knowledge, Hyde said.

"Schools need to give girls a broader view of the careers they can choose," she said. "Once girls avoid high school math, they close themselves out of fields like engineering and other fields they didn't realize involve math, and it's a shame."

Prejudice Is a Habit That Can Be Broken

Beth Azar

A Black youth sits next to you on an empty subway car. An openly gay man interviews with you for a job in your office. A Hispanic woman asks you for directions. How should you react? How *do* you react?

Few people openly admit they should or would react with prejudice to situations like these. And yet, blatant and more subtle forms of prejudice occur every day. People may withhold promotions from minority persons or may be less willing to give directions or the time of day to someone of a different race. Even people who score low on the Modern Racism Scale—a widely used test of prejudice—tend to show subtle bias when interacting with certain ethnic groups. They may avoid eye contact and physical closeness or act less friendly.

Automatic Prejudice

Some people claim that prejudice hasn't actually declined over the past 20 years, but is just better disguised. Several researchers addressed these problems and potential solutions in symposia on prejudice and stereotyping.

A powerful technique lets researchers "get inside the heads of subjects" and record subtle unconscious or unadmitted biases, said Russell Fazio, PhD, of Indiana University. The technique, called "priming," records people's subconscious reactions to stimuli. Subjects are primed by a word or picture, then asked to respond to another stimulus—often a word. For example, a prime could be the face of a white person. After

From the *APA Monitor*, October 1995, p. 28.

researchers show subjects the face, they ask them to perform certain tasks. The subjects may have to judge adjectives as positive or negative or fill in missing letters to form words.

Priming is based on the idea that thinking of a word activates a spot in the brain where the word is stored as well as connections to other words and ideas related to that word. So after seeing a prime word people access terms or ideas related to the prime faster than terms or ideas unrelated to the prime. For example, if people are primed with "dog" they will be faster at recognizing "cat" than "car." Researchers get this priming effect even if the prime is shown so quickly that the subject doesn't remember seeing it.

Researchers find prejudicial reactions in many people after numerous priming tasks—even people who claim not to be prejudiced. For example, people primed with a photo of an Asian person holding a sign that says "N__P" most often fill in the blank letter with an "i" to spell NIP—a derogatory term for Asians.

In a recent experiment, Fazio and his colleagues briefly presented high-resolution color images of Black and White faces, then had subjects identify obviously positive or negative adjectives as positive or negative by pressing one of two buttons. For example, a subject would see "attractive" and would press the "positive" button. The faster the response, the more related the adjective would be to the prime in the subjects' mind.

They found a highly significant interaction between the race of the person in the photo and the speed of subjects' reaction to positive and negative adjectives. When White subjects saw a Black face and then a negative adjective, they responded faster than when they saw a White face. The opposite occurred for positive adjectives.

On average, Whites displayed negativity toward Blacks, and vice versa, said Fazio. However, there were many individual differences, with some White subjects reacting highly negatively toward Blacks and others reacting as positively toward Blacks as Blacks themselves.

They found that the automatic responses in White subjects predicted subtle nonverbal behaviors in a 10-minute, one-on-one interaction with a Black experimenter. The experimenter rated subjects on friendliness, paying attention to such nonverbal behaviors as eye contact, personal distance, and smiling. People's scores correlated with their scores on the priming task.

These subtle prejudicial responses don't necessarily mean people will act in an openly biased fashion. Fazio and other prejudice researchers have found that some people are motivated to control overt prejudice depending on the situation. For example, people will temper their answers to the Modern Racism Scale to look less prejudiced if the interviewer is Black.

There seem to be three types of people: those who are openly prejudiced and show it in their overt and covert actions; those who believe they are not prejudiced and try to act that way, but show some covert signs of bias; and those who believe they are not prejudiced and whose covert actions show no signs of bias.

Not Just Attitude

Patricia Devine, PhD, professor of psychology at the University of Wisconsin, Madison, believes that breaking down prejudice is a process. Like every bad habit, it goes away in stages. Data indicate that automatic biased responses occur even in people who deny they're prejudiced, admits Devine. She believes peoples' responses are based on cultural stereotypes, even if they don't believe in those stereotypes. Low-prejudice people are especially vulnerable to conflict between their beliefs and unintentional responses, said Devine. She asked high- and low-prejudice people how they thought they should respond in interactions with people of different races or sexual orientation.

She then gave them a set of hypothetical interactions and asked them how they would respond in certain situations. She asked, for example, if they would feel uncomfortable being interviewed by a gay man, a Black man or a woman. As expected, low-prejudice people thought they should, and would, respond with less prejudice than high-prejudice people did.

However, many low-prejudice people admitted they would respond with more prejudice than they thought they should. When asked how subjects felt immediately after they answered the questions, low-prejudice people who saw a discrepancy between their beliefs and their actions felt guilty, annoyed, and frustrated and were critical of themselves.

The bigger the discrepancy between beliefs and actions, the more people engaged in guilt and other self-directed negative responses. She takes this as evidence that many people who claim to be unprejudiced truly don't want to be.

To test whether self-directed negative responses can help people overcome automatic prejudiced responses, she tested people's responses to racial jokes. She had subjects listen to racial jokes and had those who laughed compare their response to their beliefs about prejudice. The low-prejudice people felt guilty and, as a result, found a second set of jokes less amusing.

"The comparison activates a self-regulatory process," said Devine. "If people don't recognize the discrepancy, however, they won't feel guilt and this process won't activate." Her work shows that even people with a nonprejudice attitude often fail to bring their behaviors in line. "Prejudice appears to be a habit that can be broken," said Devine. "We need to teach people to become skilled rather than try to change their attitudes."

9 Health

Exercise Fuels the Brain's Stress Buffers

Beth Azar

Exercise may improve mental health by helping the brain cope better with stress, according to research into the effect of exercise on neurochemicals involved in the body's stress response.

Preliminary evidence suggests that physically active people have lower rates of anxiety and depression than sedentary people. But little work has focused on why that should be. So to determine how exercise might bring about its mental health benefits, some researchers are looking at possible links between exercise and brain chemicals associated with stress, anxiety, and depression.

So far there's little evidence for the popular theory that exercise causes a rush of endorphins. Rather, one line of research points to the less familiar neuromodulator, norepinephrine, which might help the brain deal with stress more efficiently.

Subduing Stress

Work in animals since the late 1980s finds that exercise increases brain concentrations of norepinephrine in brain regions involved in the body's stress response, said Rod K. Dishman, PhD, of the University of Georgia, who has conducted some experiments.

Norepinephrine is particularly interesting to researchers because 50% of the brain's supply is produced in the locus coeruleus, a brain area that connects most of the brain regions involved in emotional and stress responses. The chemical is thought to play a major role in modulating the action of other, more prevalent, neurotransmitters that play

From the *APA Monitor*, July 1996, p. 18.

a more direct role in the stress response. And although researchers are unsure of exactly how most antidepressants work, they know that some increase brain concentrations of norepinephrine.

But Mark Sothmann, PhD, of Indiana University School of Medicine, doesn't think it's a simple matter of more norepinephrine equals less stress and anxiety and therefore less depression. Instead, he and others think exercise thwarts depression and anxiety by enhancing the body's ability to respond to stress.

"Long-term exercise training potentially adjusts the responsiveness of the [stress reaction] system and makes it more efficient," said Sothmann.

Dishman found evidence for this in a study of rats' reactions to foot shock. The brain initially responds to foot shock with a burst of norepinephrine. But when rats are exposed to a prolonged session of foot shock that they can't control or escape from, brain levels of norepinephrine are depleted. As a result, when they're exposed to foot shock 24 hours later that they *can* escape from, it takes them longer to respond than it takes rats who don't have depleted norepinephrine supplies.

Dishman compared the post-shock escape response of two sets of rats: One set remained sedentary for 12 weeks before the test, while the other had 24-hour access to activity wheels. The rats that had access to the activity wheels had quicker escape times than the sedentary rats and they had higher levels of norepinephrine in the locus coeruleus.

The wheel running seems to have protected the rats from norepinephrine depletion normally caused by uncontrollable foot shock, said Dishman.

Exercise normalizes the brain's stress response, said Sothmann. So instead of reacting strongly to every situation and severely depleting the neurotransmitter supply needed for the next situation, the body reacts less strongly and keeps norepinephrine levels more steady.

For example, when people face a novel and challenging situation, it might be best to respond and react vigorously. Indeed, norepinephrine levels increase in both high-fit and low-fit people during novel stress situations.

However, if people are exposed to the same stressful situation chronically, it might be best to minimize the body's response each time, so it can conserve energy. Sothmann and his colleagues theorized that people who exercise would be better at minimizing their response to stress than those who don't.

To test this theory, they exposed 52 middle-aged men to a mental problem-solving task designed to cause stress. The task was a standard Stroop test, where people see a list of color names—red, yellow, green, blue. Each word is printed in a color different from the one it represents, and people must name the pigment of the ink, rather than read the word. The researchers further increased the difficulty of the task by playing a tape of someone repeating a list of colors.

The men represented three fitness groups: low-fit, middle-fit, and high-fit. They performed the modified Stroop test for 12 minutes on two consecutive days. On the third day, the researchers measured blood concentrations of norepinephrine while the men again performed the task. Norepinephrine levels spiked markedly higher in the low-fit men than in either the middle- or high-fit men, indicating a greater stress response, said Sothmann.

Several studies have tried to induce the same benefits in low-fit subjects by having them exercise on a treadmill several times per week for up to 16 weeks, said Sothmann. The studies have failed, implying that people need more than a few months to benefit from exercise training.

Is All Exercise Equal?

The type of exercise might also determine its benefits. In a study in rats comparing exercise to the antidepressant drug imipramine, Dishman found that unforced exercise provided more benefits than either the drug or forced exercise.

He induced a depression-like condition in rats using the drug clomipramine; they showed several behavioral signs of depression, including an impaired sex drive. He then gave one group of rats 24-hour access to a running-wheel for 12 weeks. Another group ran on a treadmill for an hour a day, six days a week for 12 weeks. A third group received imipramine for the last six days of the 12-week experimental period. And a fourth group remained sedentary and received no treatment for the 12 weeks.

The rats given imipramine showed the hallmark response to the drug: an increase in brain concentrations of norepinephrine, an increase in serotonin metabolism—another neurotransmitter associated with depression—and a decrease in the density of β-receptors—the brain-cell receptors that norepinephrine attaches to. Both exercise groups also showed these changes. But only the wheel-running rats saw increased sexual activity, the behavioral measure Dishman used to rate depression.

These results imply that "prescribing" exercise may not improve mental fitness, said Dishman. In fact, it probably isn't "fitness," per se, that provokes the neurochemical benefits seen by researchers. For example, Dishman's treadmill-trained rats exercised more and became more physically fit than wheel-running rats. However, the wheel runners received the biggest behavioral boost as measured by increased sexual activity. And research in humans finds the same trend, said Sothmann. The ultimate benefits probably result from a combination of biological and social factors, said Dishman.

Biologically, exercise seems to give the body a chance to practice dealing with stress. It forces the body's physiological systems—all of which are involved in the stress response—to communicate much more closely than usual: The cardiovascular system communicates with the renal system, which communicates with the muscular system.

And all of these are controlled by the central and sympathetic nervous systems, which also must communicate with each other. This workout of the body's communication system may be the true value of exercise, said Sothmann.

"As one becomes deconditioned, either through sedentary living or forced bed rest due to illness or injury, the physiological stress system becomes less efficient in its ability to respond to a variety of stressors," he said. "No other type of clinical intervention [for disorders like depression] forces such dynamic communication as exercise."

Computer Addictions Entangle Students

Bridget Murray

It's 4 AM and "Steve" is engulfed in the green glare of his computer screen, one minute pretending he's a ruthless mafia lord masterminding a gambling empire, the next minute imagining he's an evil sorcerer or an alien life form.

Steve, a college student, is playing a Multiple User Dungeon (MUD) game—a fictional game modeled after Dungeons and Dragons that is played by sending online messages to other players. But as he continually logs on hours, Steve finds himself sleeping through classes, forgetting his homework, and slipping into "Internet addiction"—a disorder emerging on college campuses. Affected students spend up to 40 hours to 60 hours a week in MUDs, e-mail, and chat rooms, racking up online time unrelated to their school work.

"These people stay on their computers from midnight 'til the sun comes up," said Jonathan Kandell, PhD, assistant director of the counseling center at the University of Maryland-College Park. "It becomes a downward spiral they get sucked into."

Internet addiction can afflict anyone who has easy access to the plethora of online services, but students seem especially prone to it. As universities increasingly give students their own free Internet accounts, psychologists like Kandell and Kimberly Young, PhD, of the University of Pittsburgh-Bradford, have noticed them spending larger amounts of time online, sometimes to the detriment of their social lives and studies.

"For many students this is a very real problem," says Young. "Some of them are saying it's destroying their lives."

Few students seek help for "Internet addiction" per se. But in intake interviews, many of them say they recognize that they go online to escape, university counseling centers report. Some students say they

From the *APA Monitor,* June 1996, pp. 38, 39.

feel fidgety and nervous during every minute of "offline" time and claim they go online to avoid life's pressures.

Cyberpill

Young likens Internet addiction to any other form of addiction: It becomes a problem when it interferes with other parts of peoples' lives, such as sleep, work, socializing, and exercise.

"Some of these people even forget to eat," she says.

The Internet can be a healthy, helpful tool when used to find information or to communicate with friends, coworkers, and professors, she said. But people become dependent on it when they use it mainly to fill their time, and may even lose the ability to *control* that use.

"Substitute the word 'computer' for 'substance' or 'alcohol,' and you find that Internet obsession fits the classic *Diagnostic and Statistical Manual [of Mental Disorders]* definition of addiction," says Young.

People seek the same escapist, pleasurable feelings from the Internet that they seek from drugs, gambling, or alcohol, she believes. Gambling gives them a high, alcohol numbs them, and the Internet offers them an alternate reality. Just as people struggle to keep from taking a drink or popping a pill, they struggle to turn their computer off, she said. And the Internet can serve as a tonic for students with underlying social problems, depression, or anxiety.

Paradoxically, the Internet's usefulness and social acceptability make it easy to abuse, says psychologist Kathleen Scherer, PhD, of the counseling and mental health center at the University of Texas-Austin.

Students will log on to their computer to check e-mail from a professor or to write a paper for their biology class, and then with a simple push of a button, immerse themselves in Internet banter for hours.

"It becomes so easy for students to move between work time and play time that the line between the two gets blurred," said Scherer.

Plug-in Buddy

Another danger of incessant online surfing is that Internet social interactions can start to replace real social relationships, Scherer warns.

Although some educators argue that television or reading also cut into peoples' social lives, Scherer claims the Internet is more addictive because it offers interaction with other people that ostensibly fills a social void. Stories abound about Internet addicts who lose mates, families, and friends, and about students who would rather ask strangers for dates over e-mail than approach them in person.

Students visiting chat rooms or playing MUD games can assume new, glamorous identities. Some start to believe that they're loved and cared for in their new identities—"an illusion that these online relationships are the same as the real thing," said Kandell.

"Online you have the freedom to talk to anyone, be anything you want and not be censored for it," he said. "It's a sort of unconditional acceptance unusual in flesh-and-blood relationships that makes you less used to dealing with real life."

Students sometimes attach to their computers emotionally and form a distorted view of social interactions, notes psychologist Linda Tipton, PhD, a colleague of Kandell's at Maryland. They spend the evening with their computer instead of going out and meeting people, she said.

Logging Off

Psychologists are looking for ways to help Internet junkies overcome their addiction. Hoping to attract the ones who don't come in for counseling—the majority—Tipton last fall offered a campus-wide workshop called "Caught in the Net." Only three students attended because, Tipton says, "it's hard to break through the denial and admit you have a problem."

Scherer drew a bigger audience for a workshop she hosted at the University of Texas with her husband, computer scientist Jacob Kornerup. Sixteen people, both faculty and students, attended the session, and learned how to control the amount of time they play online, for instance, by stopping their subscriptions to the online services they find most addictive. Attendees informally told Scherer that the workshop helped, and some pursued counseling for their addiction. To determine the extent of the problem at the University of Texas, Scherer and psychologist Jane Morgan Bost, PhD, assistant director of the counseling and mental health center, are conducting a study of 1,000 students, some who use the Internet and some who don't. They want to determine the forms the disorder takes and how best they can help afflicted students.

For example, some students may prefer online support services to counseling or workshops, said Scherer. Already the Internet Addiction Support Group, an Internet service recently established by psychiatrist Ivan Goldberg, MD, has begun attracting subscribers. Users of the service own up to their addiction and swap ways to tackle it.

Once addicts can say "enough is enough," and deliberately switch the computer off without regret, they're on the way to recovery, said Scherer.

"There are a lot of valuable and not-so-valuable resources on the Internet," she said. "To manage your use, you have to know the difference in value and know yourself."

Improving Quality of Life for the Seriously Ill

Tori DeAngelis

Through treatment and assessment, psychologists are helping people with life-threatening illnesses such as cancer and AIDS cope better with their conditions, boost their immune functioning, and in some cases live longer.

These are some of the findings from research on the impact of psychological treatments on patients' quality and length of life. In addition to working with cancer and AIDS patients, psychologists are also helping assess whether people are appropriate organ transplant patients.

Helping AIDS Patients

Psychological interventions are helping gay, HIV-positive men deal better with their diagnosis, said Michael Antoni, PhD, of the University of Miami. He described several studies reporting positive effects of stress-management, cognitive–behavioral, and other treatments, including several that he, Neil Schneiderman, PhD, and other colleagues at the University of Miami and in the Netherlands are conducting.

In a recent study, the Miami team assigned a group of gay men getting tested for their HIV status into two conditions: a cognitive–behavioral stress-management program and a waiting list. The stress-management treatment is aimed at raising patients' awareness of stress symptoms and helping them learn to challenge their negative thinking to better combat stress. The treatment also provided social support and bodily relaxation training, which helped them work better with their

From the *APA Monitor*, October 1995, p. 19.

thought processes. The men learned about their HIV status during the course of the intervention.

The team hypothesized that finding out one's status may lead to social isolation and poor coping strategies that could suppress the immune system. That suppression could lead to poor control of herpes viruses and ultimately to HIV replication, Antoni said.

During the trial, 31 men tested positive for HIV. As predicted, the control-group men who tested positive for HIV reported greater isolation and loneliness following their diagnosis. HIV-positive men in the intervention group, however, did not become lonelier and didn't lose social support, he said. In addition, the amount of social support people sought was linked positively or negatively to changes in natural killer cell activity, an indicator of how well the immune system is handling stress.

Compared with controls, the intervention group also had fewer levels of the Epstein-Barr virus than the control group, Antoni said, indicating they were warding off activation of these viruses. The finding is of special medical significance because the "B" cells in the body only carry receptor sites for the HIV virus if they've been infected with the E-B virus, while the "T" cells always carry those sites. In addition, when the virus gets activated under stress, it provides "several genetic opportunities to perturb HIV infection," Antoni said.

At one- and two-year follow-ups, an interesting psychological finding emerged: After a year, those able to break through their denial about having HIV had higher CD-4 counts—indicating that the disease is progressing more slowly than it otherwise might. Better program adherence—measured by the number of stress-management classes that subjects attended and how much they practiced coping strategies and cognitive exercises at home—also predicted better health, Antoni said.

Two years later, the men were still healthier than controls. In addition, men who had come to terms with their status, and who had adhered more to the intervention program, showed fewer immunological symptoms, and fewer of them developed full-blown AIDS, he said.

Help for Cancer

Interventions to improve the psychological health of cancer patients have also improved their physical health, said Barbara Andersen, PhD, of Ohio State University. Such interventions as specifically targeted group therapy and relaxation training have been shown to improve patients' moods, lower their emotional distress, and improve their ability to cope with their illnesses, she said.

Several treatment strategies are effective in helping cancer patients cope, Andersen said. They include support groups in which people with the same kind and stage of cancer can vent feelings about the illness and its treatment; providing information about the disease and letting patients respond to that information; and helping people develop behavioral and cognitive coping strategies, in particular problem-solving skills.

In groups she's run with breast-cancer patients, for instance, she's helped women think about ways to deal with fatigue and lack of time to do what they want to do.

In addition, strategies that work include progressive muscle-relaxation training and helping women identify the people who support them, and in what arenas. She then helps them mobilize that support in ways "that are likely to match their needs," Andersen said.

Immune Functioning

Few studies have been done to date that look at treatment effects on immune functioning and other health factors, Andersen said. One of the most comprehensive, by psychiatrist Fawzy Fawzy, MD, and colleagues at the University of California-Los Angeles, looks very promising, she said.

The team assigned newly treated patients with stage-one or stage-two skin cancer to either a short-term intervention group or no intervention. The intervention included fatigue management, relaxation management, and group support.

At six months, the intervention group showed significant increases in natural killer cell activity, a sign the immune system is functioning well. Six years after treatment, 29% of controls had died compared to 9% of the treated group. Survivors in the treatment group also continued to show greater numbers of killer cells and significant declines in emotional distress, she said.

In a study Andersen and colleagues at Ohio State University are now conducting on women with stage-two or stage-three breast cancer, preliminary results confirm the view that stress negatively impacts physical health. So far, they've found that women who experience more stress with their cancer diagnosis and treatment have lower natural killer-cell counts than normal. The team is also testing the effects of a psychological intervention on these women, she said.

Organ Recipients

Psychologists also help medical teams identify the best transplant candidates. According to Mary Ellen Olbrisch, PhD, of Virginia Commonwealth University, psychologists are extensively involved in assessing who is most capable of dealing with the required medical regimen. Psychologists also intervene with those who are weak on such skills, but who can develop them through behavioral change strategies and support.

To assess patients, she and a team of colleagues have developed a predictive tool that tests which patients have the psychological strength to handle the transplant process and its after-effects. The scale looks at social support, personality, mental health, lifestyle, and behavioral factors.

For candidates who have failed to change self-destructive behaviors that have often led to the need for transplant surgery, she and colleagues do what they call "behavioral contracting," Olbrisch said. The first part of that process involves helping health-care teams develop policies that can uniformly be applied to all transplant candidates, such as not smoking. Once those policies have been developed, she talks to patients about ways to change their behavior to comply with those policies.

If patients fail in their efforts to change, it can be a chance for further interventions such as intensive smoking-cessation programs. At other times, it's a chance "for the team to confirm its doubts about the patient's ability" to commit to the process, and those patients do not receive transplants.

For patients with psychological rather than behavioral problems, psychologists use psychotherapy, she said. While mental disorders such as anxiety and adjustment problems don't necessarily rule out successful transplant surgery, "they are a cause of suffering that should be treated along with other co-morbidities," Olbrisch said.

10 Stress and Adjustment

Research Looks at How Children Fare in Times of War

Erin Burnette

Children react differently to war, depending on their culture, national identity, and family and community support systems, says psychologist Mona Macksoud, PhD.

Macksoud has studied children in war zones in the Middle East, Central America, and South Africa for the last seven years. Her work, funded through the Center for the Study of Human Rights at Columbia University, focuses on understanding how war affects children's psychological health.

To gather data, Macksoud's team developed questionnaires and trained local mental health professionals to conduct clinical interviews with youth in each country.

In Lebanon, the team examined the elements that buffer children from wartime stress. Beginning in 1987, they interviewed 2,000 children and studied 300 families over five years.

They examined key protective factors that already existed in the children's families and communities, and found that children whose parents and other caregivers had high self-esteem, good morale, and a solid support system coped better with the atrocities of war and had the ability to tolerate stress.

Developmental Milestones

Macksoud also looked at developmental milestones that can serve as protective factors from wartime stress for children and youth.

For 5- to 11-year-olds, feelings of competence that stem from

From the *APA Monitor*, January 1996, p. 35.

successfully dealing with stressful life events such as divorce, sibling rivalry, competition in school, and financial difficulty, can buffer war's impact.

For 11- to 17-year olds, national identity—how children perceive their country's political ideology and their own role in the armed conflict—was the developmental milestone that protected the youth emotionally, depending on the context of the war, Macksoud said.

To study this phenomenon, Macksoud's team compared Kuwaiti children with Lebanese children, as well as how different children reacted in the same country. They studied 300 Kuwaiti youth ages 10 to 17 for a year and a half starting in 1991. To make the comparison, they examined Lebanese youngsters of the same age who they'd interviewed in their other study.

The countries underwent two very different kinds of wartime situations, Macksoud noted: Kuwait experienced a short-term occupation by an external enemy, while Lebanon suffered a chronic, internal civil war that lasted for 10 years.

Romanticized View

The Kuwaiti children who had a strong national identity suffered more than those who didn't, Macksoud found. They were angry and depressed.

"They had a very romanticized view of Kuwait, so when they were first invaded by Iraq, it was a major trauma because they had overidentified with their country," she said.

The country was rich in resources and the children had idyllic family lives. As a result, they were more traumatized than those who had a lower sense of national identity, she said.

By comparison, the Lebanese children who had strong national sentiments coped better. After being exposed to years of war, they had developed a more realistic understanding of their country's conflict, Macksoud said.

The Lebanese youth saw the purpose of the war, which allowed them to cope in a more constructive way. For instance, they joined civil movements and participated in relief work. They were actively involved in figuring out where they fit in the conflict, Macksoud said.

Adapting to War

"Children pay a huge price to survive in a war zone, but they do cope," she said. "They have their own spontaneous way of making sense of the chaos around them. The result, however, is that they tend to be vulnerable, cautious of others, pessimistic about the future, and burdened by life."

Surprisingly, children in war zones can adapt positively to their environment. Many were responsive to issues of justice, protective of younger children, sensitive to other people's suffering, and knew how to cope with the unexpected, she said.

Life in a war zone can also lead to the development of organizational skills, Macksoud said.

"Interestingly, war gives them some positive coping skills that other children don't have," she said.

Working Mothers: Happy or Haggard?

Rebecca A. Clay

Does having a job as well as a home and a family enhance a woman's health or threaten it? Research on the question is sparse but contradictory.

Research in the area has pointed to two competing hypotheses, according to Nancy L. Marshall, EdD, of Wellesley College's Center for Research on Women. One, the "scarcity hypothesis," presumes that people have a limited amount of time and energy and that women with competing demands suffer from overload and inter-role conflict. The other, the "enhancement hypothesis," theorizes that the greater self-esteem and social support people gain from multiple roles outweigh the costs. Marshall's own research supports both notions.

Based on results from two studies she recently conducted, she found that having children gives working women a mental and emotional boost that childless women of the same age lack. But having children also increases work and family strain, and indirectly increases depressive symptoms.

The reason multiple roles can be both positive and negative has to do with traditional gender roles. Despite women's movement into the paid labor force, they still have primary responsibility for the "second shift"—household work and child care.

Workload Scale

To study the area further, Ulf Lundberg, PhD, professor of biological psychology at the University of Stockholm, developed a "total workload scale." Using the scale, he has found that women typically spend much more time working at paid and unpaid tasks than men.

From the *APA Monitor*, November 1995, pp. 1, 37.

Lundberg also found that age and occupational level don't make much difference in terms of women's total workload. What does matter is whether they have children. In families without children, men and women both work about 60 hours a week.

But, said Lundberg, "as soon as there is a child in the family, total workload increases rapidly for women." In a family with three or more children, women typically spend 90 hours a week in paid and unpaid work, while men typically spend only 60 hours.

Even when women and men work the same number of hours, the fact that women typically retain the main responsibility for ensuring that household and child care tasks get done takes its toll.

Women in another of Lundberg's studies reported more psychosomatic symptoms such as anxiety, tiredness, and headaches than men. Women can't look forward to relaxing during evenings or weekends, either. That's because women have a harder time than men unwinding physiologically once they're home.

"Women's stress is determined by the interaction of conditions at home and at work, whereas men respond more selectively to situations at work," explained Lundberg, adding that men seem to be able to relax more easily once they get home.

His research found that mothers who put in overtime at their paid jobs had more stress—as measured by epinephrine levels—over the weekend than fathers, even though the fathers had worked more overtime at their jobs.

These findings come as no surprise to Gary W. Evans, PhD, of Cornell University's Department of Design and Environmental Analysis. He believes that stresses on women are cumulative, and that home and work stressors combine to put women at risk. His research suggests that women can't put out one fire and move on to the next without suffering from stressful overload.

Evans also emphasized that simply coping with stress takes a toll on women's well-being. "There's a tendency to put coping in a positive light," he noted. "But when we cope with a stressor, especially one that is incessant or difficult to control, our ability to cope with subsequent environmental demands can be impaired."

The Social Support Solution

The debate about women's multiple roles could be rendered obsolete by changes in societal expectations, many experts in the field believe.

"Individual decisions about work and family take place in a social and cultural context," said Gunn Johansson, PhD, professor of work psychology at the University of Stockholm. "Society sends encouraging or discouraging signals about an individual's choices and about the feasibility of combining work and family."

According to Johansson, these signals come not only in the form of equal employment opportunity laws, but also in the support society makes available to families. A researcher in her department, for instance, compared the plight of women managers in Sweden and the former West Germany. Although the two societies are quite similar, they differ in one important respect: Sweden offers high-quality child care to almost every family that requests it.

Preliminary results from the study show that women managers in Sweden had at least two children and sometimes more, while their German counterparts were mostly single women with no children. "These women were reading the signals from their society," Johansson said. While the German women recognized that they had to forsake family for work, the Swedish women took it as their right to combine the two roles.

"In my optimistic moments," Johansson added, "I hope that this research might provide information that would prompt politicians to provide opportunities for both women and men. Women need to feel that they have a real choice when it comes to balancing work and family life."

"Learned Optimism" Yields Health Benefits

Scott Sleek

People who learn to maintain an optimistic attitude may not only avoid depression, they may actually improve their physical health, according to a controlled study by the University of Pennsylvania's Martin Seligman, PhD, and Gregory Buchanan, PhD.

The study shows that university freshmen who participated in a workshop on cognitive coping skills reported fewer adverse physical problems and took a more active role in maintaining their health. In the study, incoming freshmen were asked to complete a questionnaire designed to reflect their overall attitudes and coping behaviors.

Seligman and Buchanan invited those students identified as the most pessimistic to participate in the study. Students were assigned to attend either the 16-hour workshop or a control group, Seligman said. Workshop participants learned to dispute their chronic negative thoughts as well as learning social and work skills that can help avert depression, he said.

After an 18-month follow-up, the preliminary findings showed 22% of the workshop participants had suffered moderate or severe depression by blind clinical diagnosis, compared to 32% of the control group subjects, Seligman said.

Also, only 7% of the workshop participants suffered from a moderate or severe anxiety disorder, compared to 15% of the control group, he added.

The workshop also seemed to bolster the physical health of the participants. They reported fewer health problems during the course of the workshop, and were more likely than control subjects to see a

From the *APA Monitor*, October 1995, p. 10.

physician for maintenance or checkup rather than wait until they became ill, Buchanan said. While the subjects were young and generally healthy, he speculated the study could be replicated using older, more vulnerable subjects.

Abnormal

Public Scrutiny Sparks Some Eating Disorders

Beth Azar

The media coverage of anorexic gymnasts and bulimic divers might make one think eating disorders are epidemic among female athletes. But recent studies find that the average rate of diagnosable eating disorders among female athletes is within rates seen among nonathlete, college-age women.

Regardless of athletic ability, women are pressured by society and the media to be thin and lean. Around 4% develop an abusive and disordered relationship with food and exercise in an attempt to control their weight.

The difference for female athletes comes from the added pressure of being in the public eye, especially in sports that judge athletes not only on their athletic skill but also on their physical appearance. Studies are beginning to determine which sports most exacerbate the strong societal messages to be thin and how training environments can be modified to counter such pressure.

The Drive for Thinness

On average athletes are more satisfied with their bodies, and feel more effective and secure with their abilities than nonathletes, said Trent Petrie, PhD, of the University of North Texas, who studies eating disorders among female athletes. But by examining how much individual sports emphasize thinness, another trend emerges. Women in "lean" sports—such as gymnastics and figure skating, which emphasize

From the *APA Monitor*, July 1996, p. 33.

thinness and body shape—tend to have a stronger drive to be thin than women in other types of sports, such as basketball and soccer.

Women in lean sports also have significantly higher rates of eating disorders than women in nonlean sports, according to studies by psychologist Donald Williamson, PhD, of Louisiana State University and others. Rates for girls in lean sports who have eating disorders average around 4%, while rates for girls in nonlean sports approach zero, Williamson found.

Pressure to Perform

To test if the girls with the eating disorders feel more pressure to be thin, Petrie categorized female athletes into six groups ranging from bulimic to those without eating disorders. Bulimics had the least satisfaction with their bodies and the most strongly held beliefs that society values thinness, he found.

According to Williamson, several risk factors interact to increase a female athlete's risk of developing an eating disorder: She perceives pressure from her sport and coach to be thin, she judges her performance negatively, and she feels anxious about her performance. These three risk factors lead to an exaggerated dissatisfaction with body size and shape, and the interaction increases the odds that an eating disorder develops. Because nonlean sports don't emphasize thinness, a major risk factor disappears, said Williamson.

Studies with male athletes support Williamson's model. Men in sports that emphasize maintaining a certain weight or physique—such as wrestling and body building—tend to develop eating disorders more than men in other sports.

Precursors of Disorders

The training climate set by coaches and parents predicts the precursors of eating disorders in gymnastics, according to evidence gathered by sport psychologist Joan L. Duda, PhD, of Purdue University.

"Gymnastics doesn't cause eating disorders," she said. "There's nothing about the balance beam or uneven bars that makes a girl develop a dysfunctional relationship with food. Instead, it becomes a motivation-related question and a 'lack of information' problem."

As part of a consultant agreement with the U.S. Gymnastics Association, Duda and nutritionist Dan Benardot, PhD, of Georgia State University, conducted four studies on elite and pre-elite gymnasts. The two pre-elite groups consisted of the 1994 and 1995 pre-elite national teams, with slightly more than 70 girls each, competing for a chance to compete in the U.S. National Championship trials. The two elite groups consisted of the 21 senior national women's gymnasts, who compete in the U.S. National trials, and the 15 senior international women's gymnasts, who represent the United States in international competition. The researchers found that a training climate that emphasizes winning above all else predicted low self-esteem, negative body image, a lower degree of enjoyment, and a higher degree of stress associated with competing—the same factors Williamson and others have linked to an increased risk of eating disorders.

Gymnasts in such performance-focused environments tended to be energy deficient: They weren't eating enough to sustain their activity level. Training climates with a lowered emphasis on winning, and more emphasis on improving skills and having fun, predicted the opposite outcomes for the gymnasts. Such training climates were more common than the more risky climates. And the majority of gymnasts were happy, well-adjusted, well-nourished and free of the psychological precursors of eating disorders.

Yet the emphasis on small, thin athletes remains a problem, agreed Duda and Petrie. Although Petrie found no higher rate of diagnosable eating disorders among 200 college-level gymnasts, he discovered that more than half engaged in disordered behavior such as unnecessary dieting, fasting, and overexertion to burn calories.

Researchers need to educate coaches, parents, athletes, and judges about the risks of eating disorders and the benefits of good nutrition, said Duda. For example, when a gymnast develops an energy deficit, her metabolism slows down and she has to eat less to maintain the same weight. Besides being clinically dangerous, such a cycle is counterproductive in the long run because these girls develop higher concentrations of fat, said Duda.

The training establishment also needs to better understand the interplay between mental and physical health, she said. "If a kid is going into the gym hungry after a full day of school and [eating] no food since lunch," she said, "coaches shouldn't be surprised when during the last two hours of a four-hour practice the kid's attention span is limited, she's cranky and she's crying after every little mistake."

Paths That Lead to Teenage Depression

Beth Azar

Making one's way through adolescence is like maneuvering a mine field: Each mine represents something that can throw a kid off track. While multiple paths lead to safety and normal development, other passages lead to developmental problems.

Jeanne Brooks-Gunn, PhD, and her colleagues at Columbia University are trying to identify the mines and developmental pathways that can lead to emotional problems in girls. Researchers find large increases in depressed mood during adolescence; girls seem to lose the ability to regulate their emotions—what Brooks-Gunn called emotional dysregulation.

Brooks-Gunn is particularly interested in transitions into and out of adolescence. Earlier work showed that between age 12 and 14, girls report a host of negative life events that coincide with increases in negative emotions.

"What we see is a pile up of events occurring right around the transition into adolescence," said Brooks-Gunn.

Her studies look at the impact of hormonal changes during puberty as well as family and school stresses on girls' moods to determine how mood at one age may impact mood later in life.

The Role of Hormones

Brooks-Gunn began looking at how changes in estradiol hormone levels affect emotional dysregulation. As girls enter puberty, estradiol levels rise sharply over a few years until they reach adult levels. Brooks-Gunn

From the *APA Monitor*, October 1995, p. 26.

and her colleagues put girls in four estradiol categories—category one represents prepuberty levels, categories two and three represent early and late stage increases during puberty, and category four represents adult levels. They found the highest levels of emotional dysregulation or depressive affect in girls in category three when hormone levels were rising fastest.

"When the [hormonal] system is being activated and going up fairly rapidly, that's the time at which we were seeing some hormonal effects on emotional state," said Brooks-Gunn.

However, they found an even bigger effect on mood from negative life events. "You're seeing from 2% to 4% of the variance from hormone changes versus 8% to 18% for negative life events," said Brooks-Gunn. The hormone effect "seems to be a stable effect, but a small effect."

Those results speak to the complexity of the developmental pathway, said Brooks-Gunn. For emotions, there's an intersection of social events and hormonal events and researchers can't look at one without the other.

In another line of research, Brooks-Gunn is looking at whether problems with emotion regulation early on set kids on a trajectory for problems in adulthood. She's followed 120 girls for eight years, taking measurements at early adolescence (age 14), midadolescence (age 16), and young adulthood (age 22). At each lifestage, she separated the girls into two categories: those with and those without depressive problems. She also measured physical development, including percent body fat and onset of menarche; psychopathology, including internalizing and externalizing behavior; and peer and family relationships.

In general, she found a slight peak in depressive problems in midadolescence—26% compared with 18% for early adolescents and 16% for early adults. She then formed four categories based on data from early and midadolescence: (a) positive—girls who didn't show depressive problems at either lifestage; (b) early transient—girls who showed depressive problems in early adolescence, but not midadolescence; (c) late transient—girls who showed depressive problems in midadolescence, but not early adolescence; and (d) recurrent—girls who showed depressive problems at both points. Most girls (65%) landed in the positive category, while the other categories each averaged around 10%.

Brooks-Gunn used these categories to look for differences among the girls at each age. Recurrent girls had higher percent body fat at all times. Fourteen-year-olds with depressive problems—those who later became early transient or recurrent—had poorer body images. Recurrent girls had higher body fat and slightly earlier ages of menarche onset. Late transient girls who went on to become depressed in midadolescence had more family conflict in early adolescence. Sixteen-year-old girls with depressive problems—late transient or recurrent—had poor body images and poor adjustment. Recurrently depressed girls have more conflict with parents and poor peer relationships.

"The recurrent girls are starting to look somewhat socially isolated by age 16," said Brooks-Gunn.

Unexpected Findings

Surprisingly, girls with recurrent problems in adolescence showed only slightly higher rates of depressive problems at age 22 and the differences were barely significant, said Brooks-Gunn. To find out why, the team analyzed the results further.

First, they looked at two subgroups: girls who had depressive problems at some point in adolescence, but "bounced back" by age 22, and recurrent girls who still had problems at age 22. They found that recurrent girls had much higher internalizing and externalizing scores in midadolescence. Her guess is that these recurrent girls would be considered co-morbid with either anxiety or aggressive problems.

They then compared girls who showed signs of depressive problems at age 22 but not during adolescence with girls who didn't show signs of depressive problems at any time. They found that girls who became depressed at age 22 had more negative school and family life events in midadolescence. So new cases of depression looked more situational than recurrent cases, said Brooks-Gunn.

"This really parallels the clinical literature in showing that there seem to be very different pathways for different patterns of recurrent and chronic behavior problems," said Brooks-Gunn.

She believes her study results point to a need for intervention programs that work with girls at risk for depression.

Unlocking the Restrictions on Drinking

Scott Sleek

In a city where substance abuse pervades the homegrown, faddish "grunge" music crowd, Seattle psychologist Alan Marlatt, PhD, is espousing a philosophy that many of his colleagues regard as a dangerously ironic approach to chemical-addiction treatment.

For more than a decade, Marlatt has asserted that some problem drinkers can learn to moderate their consumption rather than stop it altogether. He contends his approach attracts patients who would otherwise go untreated, because they eschew traditional, abstinence-oriented recovery approaches. And many of those who begin treatment with moderation as a goal eventually decide on abstinence anyway, he said.

"It's amazing how many people who think they can't stop drinking do," said Marlatt, who directs the University of Washington's Addictive Behavior Research Center. "About a third never start again."

Marlatt is among a number of psychologists who advocate a more eclectic approach to treatment for alcoholism and other forms of substance abuse and dependency. He calls his technique "harm reduction," because it allows the drinker to move to a less harmful form of consumption, either on the way or as an alternative to abstinence. Such controversial ideas have circulated through the addiction-treatment fields for decades, but have sparked renewed clamor in the last several months based in part on a sudden storm of popular-media coverage.

Critics say the approach is dangerous because it could mislead many severe alcoholics to think they can safely moderate their intake. But proponents say providing a variety of treatment options—rather than a one-size-fits-all abstinence strategy—will bring otherwise resistant patients into treatment.

From the *APA Monitor*, June 1995, p. 23.

The views of Marlatt and other addiction experts expand on the traditional definitions of alcoholism, and raise a practical disagreement about the appropriate methods of helping people overcome substance-abuse problems.

Debating the Definition

Many addiction experts say the medical profession's decision several years ago to declare alcoholism a physiological disease has omitted the idea that some excessive drinking may merely be a symptom of a deeper problem, such as depression or stress. The fourth edition of the American Psychiatric Association's *Diagnostic and Statistical Manual of Mental Disorders* distinguishes alcohol dependency—physiological addiction—from alcohol abuse, which usually takes the form of episodic excessive drinking. Some psychologists complain that treatment for alcohol problems is geared toward those who are severely alcohol-dependent, even though many alcohol abusers, such as college students or party-hopping socialites, fall short of the diagnostic criteria for alcoholism.

"There are four-to-five times as many problem drinkers in the United States as there are alcoholics," said the University of New Mexico's Reid Hester, PhD, a clinical psychologist who runs an alcohol self-control program in Albuquerque. "But they don't come to the attention of the traditional alcoholism-treatment programs."

Although many of these individuals may be worried about their drinking habits, they avoid treatment because they believe abstinence programs are the only help available. Experts note that some reject the notion that they have a disease, while others shun the spiritually based philosophy of the 12-step recovery programs such as Alcoholics Anonymous. More problem drinkers would try to overcome their problem if they could find more agreeable treatment options, Marlatt said.

Market forces also have spurred the interest in alternative treatments. The drive to contain health-care costs have prompted insurers to question the expensive treatment programs and to demand proof that those methods work. In a chapter of *The Handbook of Alcoholism Treatment Approaches: Effective Alternatives,* edited by Hester and University of New Mexico psychologist William R. Miller, PhD, researchers say outcomes research shows no single treatment to be effective for *all* alcohol problems.

Tapered Consumption

Marlatt admits that the controlled-drinking approach is only appropriate with some clients. Studies show that those who are younger, regularly employed, and have more modest symptoms of problem drinking are better suited for moderation therapy, while those who show severe signs of dependency should probably strive for abstinence in their recovery. Psychologists can use screening and assessment tools to determine the appropriate treatment plan for each patient, he said.

Research indicates that patients will more likely adhere to a treatment goal of their own choosing. Alternatives include a trial abstinence period followed by controlled drinking, or a gradual tapering of consumption with abstinence as the end goal.

In a meta-analysis of the literature on treatment outcomes for alcohol problems, Miller, Hester, and several other researchers found that the intensive, traditional interventions—such as the 12-step program—are no more universally effective than less expensive, alternative treatments. Marlatt cites studies of subjects who significantly reduced, but continued their drinking through such interventions as self-management counseling.

The tailored-treatment concept may work for treating other forms of chemical addiction, Marlatt said, adding that he lives in the appropriate setting for investigating that possibility. Seattle is the center of the grunge rock scene, and heroin is said to be the drug of choice among many of its celebrities and fans.

Science or Fantasy?

The argument for moderation-training dates back to the early 1960s, when the late D. L. Davies, MD, a British physician and alcohol researcher, published the results of a study showing that a few patients treated for alcoholism eventually returned to normal or controlled drinking. Subsequent studies appear to bolster Davies' conclusions, but many of them have been challenged as flawed or even fraudulent. Critics say follow-up investigations showed most of the subjects eventually regressed into problematic drinking.

Some of the alternative treatments receive praise even from practitioners who remain loyal to the abstinence model. Marlatt's relapse prevention program, for example, shows some strong promise, said Robert Margolis, PhD, a director of the Ridgeview Action Center, an addiction treatment facility in Smyrna, Georgia.

But Margolis and other practitioners say the controlled-drinking success stories are grossly exaggerated, noting that other studies have shown people who reported initial success with moderation eventually returning to destructive drinking habits.

"In the clinical world, we rarely see sustained, controlled drinking in people who are clear alcoholics," said psychologist John Wallace, PhD, who ran the now-defunct Edgehill Newport alcoholism treatment center in Rhode Island. "The vast majority of people who are diagnosed as alcohol dependent are not able to moderate their drinking."

The controlled-drinking debate also raises concerns about the reputation of psychologists, who must compete with lesser-trained social workers and addiction counselors, Margolis said.

"It's been unfortunate that psychologists in particular have been associated with the controlled-drinking model," Margolis said. "It keeps us from being taken seriously at most treatment centers."

And because the concepts of psychologists like Marlatt and Hester have yet to reach sweeping acceptance, those who adopt such an approach could face some precarious liability risks, experts say.

"If you have an alcoholic under your care and teach him controlled drinking and he goes out and kills someone while drunk, either through drunk driving or violence, you've got a tremendous problem on your hands," Wallace said.

The dissension runs deep. Marlatt has received substantial mail from detractors; one critic even accused him of murder.

Hester said that while he believes other psychologists are realizing that substance abuse and its treatment lie on a continuum, the traditional thinking will take a long time to erode.

"People still misunderstand and think we're out to teach diabetics that they can eat sugar," he said. "I know of no one who advocates teaching moderation strategies to alcohol-dependent clients."

12 Treatment

Strong Feelings of Shame Fuel Teen Conduct Disorders

Tori DeAngelis

Two novel projects propose ways to help angry, rebellious teens live healthier lives, and to help their families gain relief and insight as well.

In one project, Fuller Theology Seminary graduate students Staci Renee Emerson Coons and Judy Kim are conducting group therapy and research with 12- to 16-year-olds diagnosed with conduct disorder. Young people with the disorder violate social rules and others' rights —sexual, property, and other.

The core of the team's treatment is psychodynamic: Drawing from object-relations theory, Coons and Kim posit that shame underlies these young people's behavior, and they work to address and heal those feelings.

Teens with conduct disorder are "exquisitely vulnerable to shame" because they have such a fragile sense of self, Kim said. They dissociate from that shame and push it onto others. This dissociation, combined with difficulty building relationships, can result in aggressive, remorseless behavior.

Healing the Shame That Binds

In two recent intervention studies, Coons and Kim ran 10-session groups once a week with small groups of these teens. They separated the groups by gender to help reduce the shame that can arise between adolescent boys and girls. Each session included a 10-minute talk on the dynamics of shame, and a 50-minute discussion group.

From the *APA Monitor*, October 1996, p. 42.

In the meetings, the team emphasized an atmosphere of validation and respect, Coons said. "These kids are used to being punished and told not to do things, and we wanted them to have a different experience," she said. "The primary goal of treatment was to give them the tools to deal internally with shame through attachments within the group and through mirroring with therapists in the group."

At the end of the 10 weeks, the young people's distorted feelings of shame dropped dramatically, as measured on the Internalized Shame Scale.

The girls' scores fell lower than the boys', Kim added.

"For adolescent girls, it's probably more acceptable to express their experience of shame, and so they stand a greater chance of healing from it," she suggested.

STAND-UP

As head of a project that takes a different tack on risky teen behavior, David Castro-Blanco, PhD, of the Long Island Jewish Medical Center's Division of Child and Adolescent Psychiatry, described a cognitive–behavioral intervention he has developed for such adolescents.

In Strategic Treatment for Adolescents, through Negotiated Decision-Making, Using Positives (STAND-UP), Castro-Blanco uses negotiated decision-making and conflict-resolution techniques to help teens and their families interact more effectively.

Castro-Blanco thinks of teens' high-risk behaviors as "extreme behavioral responses to interpersonal conflicts, frequently occurring within the family," he said. So he aims through the 10-week program to meet these conflicts head on and to help families and teens address them effectively. In the process, he helps the young people develop stronger coping, problem-solving, and communication skills.

In the first session, Castro-Blanco establishes a positive working atmosphere by encouraging youngsters and their families to elicit positive statements about each other. This strategy "facilitates us [sic] being able to do a lot of other work with the family," Castro-Blanco said.

He uses "gizmos" at this stage to facilitate the process, including "Social Tokens" that youngsters and families give to each other to express appreciation, and a "Feeling Thermometer" that allows teens to gauge the degree of anger they feel. The thermometer "is like a smoke detector—it alerts adolescents and their families that there's a crisis brewing," Castro-Blanco said.

In the next phase of the intervention, he helps the family discuss factors that promote family problems, and to develop a consensus on them. For example, a teen may say his parents give him no freedom or respect, while the parents feel "the kid can't be trusted as far as they can throw a grand piano," Castro-Blanco joked. He helps them develop a compromise, such as letting the teen go out with friends after completing specific chores.

He also encourages families to listen to one another. To counter the tendency to tune each other out, for example, he has family members act out the parts of other family members, so they get an inside view of how others feel.

"If you're able to start listening to what each other wants, you're more likely to get what you want heard, too," he said.

In the last phase of the program, Castro-Blanco helps families assess the effectiveness of their negotiations, and determine how to maintain them. "The goal is to help the family be their own best therapists," Castro-Blanco said.

Castro-Blanco is putting the intervention into a manual format, and collecting data on its effectiveness.

Nursing Marriage From Sickness to Health

Beth Azar

Four years ago, newlyweds Susan and Dave moved into a town house in the Washington, DC, suburbs. They shared a courtyard with six other young couples, each as happy as the next. Today, only Susan and Dave and one other couple are still married. And Susan is left wondering what happened.

Their neighborhood is a casualty of changing times, say marriage researchers. Relationships between men and women are evolving faster than many marriages can withstand. As a result, the divorce rate hovers around 50%, more people are postponing or opting out of marriage, and even more are deciding to live together without marrying, at least at first.

Even so, most people want to be in a romantic relationship and keep trying despite the dismal statistics, and psychologists are examining what makes marriages fail and ways to help them work.

Problems With Equality

Most marriage researchers agree that women's new roles in society have precipitated changes in marriage and the rise in divorce.

"There has been a world-wide revolution in women's rights both economic and psychological," said psychologist John Gottman, PhD of the University of Washington. "And as the rate of women working increased, so did divorce rates."

Today, almost 60% of wives work and 22.3% of them earn more than their husbands. The change in women's work status not only forces

From the *APA Monitor*, September 1995, pp. 10, 11.

more egalitarian marriages, but decreases pressures for women to marry or stay in a bad marriage—they can be financially independent and remain unmarried without stigma.

But women working doesn't cause divorce. Working actually increases women's satisfaction at home, said psychologist and marriage researcher Howard Markman, PhD, of the University of Denver. What decreases their satisfaction and precipitates divorce are the problems they face communicating and negotiating with their husbands, many of whom may be put off by their wives' careers or stuck in traditional views of spousal roles.

"Equality puts a premium on negotiating everything," said psychologist Clifford Notarius, PhD, of Catholic University and author with Markman of *We Can Work It Out: Making Sense of Marital Conflict.* "Meanwhile, the problem with most couples is that they don't know how to discuss conflict."

He and other marriage researchers have begun to design programs to help couples learn how to come to terms with their new roles and negotiate the inevitable conflict that will arise.

The Future of Marriage

Another consequence of gender equality and individualism is an overall decline in how many people marry. The number of unmarried adults nearly doubled between 1970 and 1993, from 37.5 million to 72.6 million, according to U.S. Census Bureau statistics. More than half of this group have never married.

Those who do marry are postponing it longer than they have since 1890: The average age at first marriage for women rose from 21.3 in 1960 to 24.5 in 1993 and for men from 22.8 in 1960 to 26.5 in 1993.

At the same time, the number of unmarried couples living together rose 454% since 1970 to 2.9 million couples in 1990. By age 34, 45% of adults have co-habitated and 39% of married couples lived with their spouse before marriage.

But living together before the nuptials is no guarantee of marital success. In fact, couples who live together first divorce at higher rates than couples who live separately before marriage—38% and 27% respectively within 10 years, according to one study by University of Wisconsin researchers.

Part of the problem may be that the "institution" of cohabitation isn't well structured, said sociologist Steven Nock, PhD, of the University of Virginia. Marriage is a normative relationship—there are special terms for married couples and a recognized relationship between spouses, their families, and friends.

Cohabitation, however, has no normative terms or roles. Lovers who live together are less committed to their relationships, tend to be less religious, more independent, and have less traditional views of marriage and sex roles. They often have strained relationships with their parents and their partner's parents, said Nock.

A Biological Need

Even with these trends away from marriage, it's still very popular. People cite marriage as one of the most important sources of happiness and 90% marry at least once by the time they're 50, said Notarius.

"People want to share their life with someone," he said. "They're looking for an intimate relationship that provides comfort, sexual gratification, and friendship with a life-long partner."

It's a universal biologically driven need to give and receive care, note psychologists Elaine Hatfield, PhD, and Richard Rapson, PhD, of the University of Hawaii in their book *Love and Sex: Cross-Cultural Perspectives* (1995). They cite historical, sociological, and psychological data from around the world, indicating the common thread of love and relationships throughout history.

There are also many *logical* reasons to marry, said Gottman. For one, there are big economic advantages, especially for people who want to raise a family. Also, research shows that a two-parent family is still the best place to raise kids, especially if the father is emotionally engaged.

"The benefits of marriage are extraordinary," said Notarius. "If you look at utilization of medical and psychiatric resources, happily married couples use less than any one else in the population. People are aware of the benefits a good marriage can provide."

Besides, few people think they'll be one of the statistics, say researchers. When psychologist Blaine Fowers, PhD, asked married couples what their chance of divorce is, the average answer was 10% and more than three fourths refused to acknowledge it was even a remote possibility.

Lofty Expectations

Fantasies about marriage and the likelihood of divorce can contribute to matrimonial discord, said Fowers, of the University of Miami.

He studies marital illusions—the fantasies and unrealistic ideas people hold about marriage in general and their partners in particular. He found that happy couples are more likely to form illusions than unhappy couples. They agree to unrealistically rosy descriptions of their marriage. And they idealize their spouses, attributing more positive qualities to them than to anyone else and giving their spouses credit for more positive aspects of the marriage than themselves.

In other words, the higher the level of marital satisfaction, the more marital illusions are in place, said Fowers. This implies that, to be happy in a marriage, people must form unrealistic illusions.

This trend seems particularly salient in the United States. When Hatfield asked college students in the United States, Japan, and Russia what traits they desired in a mate, students in the three countries gave surprisingly similar answers. They cited such traits as kindness and understanding, a sense of humor, expressiveness and openness and intelligence (in that order). However, more so than students in Russia and Japan, American students assumed they could, and should, ''have it all'' from their partner.

''We have to engage in illusions to maintain the kind of satisfaction we expect,'' said Fowers. ''When problems arise, the illusions break down and people become dissatisfied.''

One way to deal with this dilemma is to form a broader sense of a good marriage, said Fowers. Instead of thinking in terms of individual satisfaction, people need to start thinking about family as a unit rather than the sum of its parts, he said.

What Treatments Have Proven Effective?

Scott Sleek

Psychologists are no longer satisfied asking the simple self-explorative question, "Does psychotherapy work?" Instead, research on psychotherapy has expanded in focus, examining the *extent* to which therapy helps people, whether any treatments are more effective than others, and whether a therapist's level of training affects patient outcomes. Although a variety of clinical researchers and theorists disagree about whether the profession has truly proven the extent to which therapy works, all agree that the research focus has indeed become more intricate.

"We have to go to the kind of specificity where we ask, for a given kind of issue or problem, what specific kind of operationalized intervention, applied flexibly and clinically, is effective," said David Barlow, PhD, who runs the Phobia and Anxiety Disorders Clinic at the State University of New York at Albany. "I don't think any other kind of analysis makes any sense anymore."

Indeed, third-party payers, which for years have challenged psychologists to produce data showing their treatment outcomes, are already establishing more detailed indicators of clinical effectiveness.

Does Psychotherapy Work?

Numerous studies show that the effects of psychosocial treatments, either alone or along with medical or pharmacological care, clearly exceed those of other interventions, for ailments ranging from panic disorder to schizophrenia, Barlow said. A recent study showed that, when

From the *APA Monitor*, October 1995, pp. 40, 42.

research subjects are followed long term, they show an ability to effectively deal with the inevitable, symptomatic recurrences of their psychological disorders, he added.

"They do seem to have benefitted from having the psychological treatment in that they are able to deal more effectively with these exacerbations and remissions," he said.

But in a debate with Barlow about psychotherapy's scientific base, Andrew Christensen, PhD, psychology professor at the University of California, Los Angeles, argued that psychologists have only been able to prove that therapy delivers modest benefits. Christensen claimed that past comparisons between psychological interventions and medical treatment have been methodologically flawed. For example, while life or death is often the standard of success for medical care, psychotherapy researchers often label psychological treatments successful if patients improve their score on a questionnaire or psychological test—even by a few points, he said.

Researchers have pegged the success rate for psychotherapy at 70% to 80%, compared with no more than 30% for addiction treatment, he said. But the criteria for addiction treatment success is much more stringent and precise, with abstinence being the basic measure of success, he noted.

"If you're treating cocaine abusers, they're not counted as improved if they increase their self-esteem a little bit," he said.

Christensen also pointed to a well-known National Institute of Mental Health study involving more than 200 patients being treated for depression. In an 18-month follow-up, the study found that no more than 30% of the subjects had recovered from depressive symptoms and experienced no relapse.

Barlow argued that the NIMH study involved several sites, which creates an inherent blemish. Based on his own experience with multisite studies, he pointed to the difficulty of ensuring that all the clinicians at various sites administer the treatment under study in a consistent, competent manner.

Who and What Works Best?

Research largely indicates no link between professional training and the quality of treatment delivered, Christensen argued. In fact, a review earlier this year of 150 studies of psychotherapy with children and adolescents indicated that paraprofessionals—typically parents or teachers trained in specific intervention methods—demonstrated larger treatment effects than student therapists or fully trained mental health-care professionals, he said. (Typically these parents and teachers were trained in methods developed by mental health professionals, he noted.)

Most studies have found no consistent differences between treatment approaches, Christensen said. In fact, research at the University of Alabama showed that subjects suffering from depression improved just by reading the popular self-help book *Feeling Good* by psychiatrist David Burns, MD, he said.

The therapy often does not impact the problem it targeted, he added. One study found that subjects who demonstrated the largest benefit from cognitive therapy were those who were the least cognitively impaired from the outset, he said.

"We're far from the notion of specific treatments for specific problems," he said.

Barlow said research is starting to show some distinctions in the quality of therapy and outcomes. One study showed that quality psychotherapy proved nearly as effective as medication in preventing relapse of major depressive episodes three years post-treatment, while patients who received therapy of less quality almost all relapsed in the time period, he said.

The treatments that are supported in clinical studies often prove even more successful when used in everyday practice, Barlow added. Nationwide results of panic disorder treatment indicate that practitioners are achieving a 90% success rate, compared to 70% achieved in clinical studies, he said.

Practitioners often take a more flexible approach when using research-supported treatments, attending to a patient's peripheral issues—such as the death of a loved one—in addition to the specific disorder being treated, he said.

"We think they take what we develop and integrate it in a common sense way into their practice, paying attention to the kinds of clinical issues that come up from time to time," he said. "We don't have that luxury in our research."

A Difficult Endeavor

Clinical researchers acknowledge other necessary directions for outcomes research, such as a better accounting for comorbidity in research subjects. (Most patients in the clinical world often are diagnosed with and treated for more than one disorder.)

But overall, outcomes research has proven psychotherapy to be effective, said Ken Howard, PhD, a Northwestern University psychology professor and a leading scholar on psychotherapy outcomes. The literature, he said, contains about 1,000 studies on the effectiveness of psychotherapy. But Howard also noted that psychotherapy is held to a higher standard of accountability than other professions, for the following reasons: (a) The mental health profession encompasses a variety of disciplines, including social work and nursing, leading to turf battles rather than a cohesive professional advocacy group to represent the field; (b) beneficiaries of psychologists' services—namely, the patients and their families—won't form a grassroots advocacy group to tout therapy's worth because of confidentiality concerns; and (c) practitioners have developed a plethora of theories on therapy, and some seem farfetched to the public.

Howard also pointed out that various parties have different expectations of therapy outcomes. For example, most clients say they're satisfied with therapy, but third-party payers don't trust client self-reports and instead ask the clinician whether the patient has returned to normal functioning at home and work, he said.

Studies also indicate that psychotherapy is also not the only hope for emotional problems or disorders, but may simply expedite an individual's recovery or improvement, Howard noted.

"We're seeing that therapy accomplishes in 16 sessions what the patient accomplishes on his own in two year's time," he said. "Winning the lottery is very therapeutic. Falling in love is very therapeutic. Therapy just offers a pure culture of that."

About the Editors

Jill N. Reich, PhD, is the Executive Director for Education at the American Psychological Association (APA). She has served as Dean of the Faculty at Trinity College in Hartford, Connecticut; Director and Chairperson of the Loyola University (Chicago) Psychology Department; and Director for the Loyola University Center for Children and Families. Dr. Reich is the recipient of the APA Distinguished Contributions to Education in Psychology Award and the APA Centennial Award for Early Career Contributions to Education and Training. A graduate of Dartmouth College in Developmental Psychology, Dr. Reich has authored books, chapters, and numerous journal articles on child development.

Elizabeth Q. Bulatao, Communications Development Officer in the Office of Communications, American Psychological Association, provides technical assistance and manages special projects. She previously managed special projects in child psychiatry, and international projects in women's health and family planning for development agencies. She has written on such topics as workplace violence, U.S. government initiatives in managed care, and developing-country family planning programs. Ms. Bulatao has a master's degree in sociology from Loyola University, Chicago.

Gary R. VandenBos, PhD, is the Executive Director, Publications and Communications of the American Psychological Association, where he manages the APA knowledge dissemination program—APA Journals, APA Books, and PsycINFO. He is an associate editor of the *American Psychologist,* managing editor of *Professional Psychology: Research and Practice,* and contributing editor for *Psychiatric Services.* He has taught at

Michigan State University and the University of Bergen (Norway). Among Dr. VandenBos's major interests is the translation of psychological research knowledge into application—in training, in treatment, in public policy, and in disseminating scholarly information within psychology and to the public.

Rhea K. Farberman is the Associate Executive Director for Public Communications, American Psychological Association. In her position she directs the Association's media relations program, runs its in-house small publications department, and is the Executive Editor of the *APA Monitor*, APA's monthly newsmagazine. An accredited member of the Public Relations Society of America (PRSA), Ms. Farberman is a member of the Board of Directors of PRSA's Health Care Academy. She is a 1982 graduate of The American University School of Communications and completed graduate studies in public relations at The George Washington University.